Contents

22

36

25

8

Summer Celebrations

Quick, crowd-pleasing summer sweets perfect for picnics, reunions, barbecues, and block parties

 ## Classic S'mores

Total: 5 minutes

- 4 **JET-PUFFED** Marshmallows, toasted
- 1 milk chocolate candy bar (1.55 ounces), quartered
- 4 **HONEY MAID** Honey Grahams, broken in half (8 squares)

SANDWICH 1 toasted marshmallow and 1 chocolate piece between each of 2 graham squares to make each s'more.

Makes 4 servings, 1 s'more each.

- - - - - - - - - -

USE YOUR MICROWAVE: Make indoor s'mores! Top each of 4 graham squares with 1 chocolate piece and 1 untoasted marshmallow. Place on microwaveable plate. Microwave on HIGH 15 to 20 seconds or until marshmallows puff. Top each with a second graham square; press together gently to secure.

Red, White & Blueberry Parfaits

15 Minute Prep

Total: 4 hours 15 minutes (includes refrigeration)

1 cup boiling water

1 package (4-serving size) **JELL-O** Strawberry Flavor Sugar Free Low Calorie Gelatin, or any other red flavor

1 cup cold water

1 tub (8 ounces) **COOL WHIP LITE** Whipped Topping, thawed, divided

1½ cups blueberries

STIR boiling water into dry gelatin mix in medium bowl at least 2 minutes until completely dissolved. Stir in cold water. Pour into 13×9-inch pan.

REFRIGERATE 4 hours or until firm.

CUT gelatin into ½-inch cubes. Reserve 1 cup of the whipped topping for garnish. Layer blueberries, remaining whipped topping and the gelatin cubes in 8 dessert glasses. Top with the reserved whipped topping. Store in refrigerator.

Makes 8 servings.

- - - - - - - - - -

SUBSTITUTE: Prepare as directed, using COOL WHIP Sugar Free Whipped Topping.

Key Lime Margarita Pie

Total: 6 hours 15 minutes (includes freezing)

1 ¼   cups crushed pretzels

¼   cup sugar

6   tablespoons butter or margarine, melted

1   can (14 ounces) sweetened condensed milk

½   cup lime juice

1   envelope **KOOL-AID** Lemon Lime Unsweetened Soft Drink Mix

1   tub (8 ounces) **COOL WHIP** Whipped Topping, thawed, divided

MIX crushed pretzels, sugar and butter. Press firmly onto bottom and up side of 9-inch pie plate. Refrigerate until ready to fill.

COMBINE condensed milk, lime juice and drink mix in large bowl until well blended. Remove ½ cup whipped topping; refrigerate until ready to use. Gently stir in remaining whipped topping. Pour into crust.

FREEZE 6 hours or overnight. Let stand at room temperature 15 minutes or until pie can be cut easily. Garnish with reserved whipped topping before serving. Store leftover pie in freezer.

Makes 10 servings.

JAZZ IT UP: For added lime flavor, stir in 2 tablespoons grated lime peel with lime juice.

Peach & Raspberry Trifle

Total: 2 hours 25 minutes (includes refrigerating)

3	tablespoons orange juice
¼	teaspoon almond extract
1	package (9 ounces) prepared angel food cake, cut into 1-inch cubes
1	pound ripe peaches, peeled, divided
¼	cup raspberry fruit spread
2	cups raspberries, divided
2¾	cups fat free milk
2	packages (4-serving size each) **JELL-O** Vanilla Flavor Fat Free Sugar Free Instant Reduced Calorie Pudding & Pie Filling
1½	cups thawed **COOL WHIP LITE** Whipped Topping, divided

COMBINE orange juice and almond extract. Drizzle over cake cubes in large bowl; toss lightly. Set aside. Slice peaches; set aside. Mix fruit spread with 1 cup of the raspberries.

POUR milk into separate large bowl. Add dry pudding mixes. Beat with wire whisk 2 minutes or until well blended. Gently stir in 1 cup of the whipped topping.

PLACE half of the cake cubes in 2-quart glass serving bowl or round baking dish. Top with layers of half each of the raspberries, peaches and pudding mixture. Top with remaining cake cubes, remaining raspberries, peaches and remaining pudding mixture; cover with plastic wrap. Refrigerate at least 2 hours. Top with remaining ½ cup whipped topping just before serving. Store leftover dessert in refrigerator.

Makes 16 servings, ½ cup each.

- - - - - - - - - -

MAKE AHEAD: Trifle can be made up to 6 hours in advance.

Citrus Sorbet Pie

Total: 4 hours 20 minutes (includes freezing)

⅔ cup boiling water

1 package (4-serving size) **JELL-O** Orange Flavor Gelatin

1 cup orange sherbet

2 cups thawed **COOL WHIP** Whipped Topping

2 cups **JET-PUFFED** Miniature Marshmallows

1 can (8 ounces) crushed pineapple, drained

1 **HONEY MAID** Graham Pie Crust (6 ounces)

STIR boiling water into dry gelatin mix in large bowl at least 2 minutes until completely dissolved. Add sherbet; stir until sherbet is completely melted and mixture is slightly thickened. Add whipped topping, marshmallows and pineapple; stir gently with wire whisk until well blended. Refrigerate 10 minutes or until mixture is very thick and will mound.

POUR into crust.

FREEZE 4 hours or until firm. Store leftover pie in freezer.

Makes 8 servings.

- - - - - - - - -

VARIATION: Prepare as directed, using JELL-O Lime Flavor Gelatin and lemon sherbet.

Easy Chocolate Éclair Squares

Total: 3 hours 30 minutes (includes refrigerating)

1¾ cups cold milk

1 package (4-serving size) **JELL-O** Vanilla Flavor Instant Pudding & Pie Filling

1 tub (8 ounces) **COOL WHIP** Whipped Topping, thawed

22 **HONEY MAID** Honey Grahams

3 tablespoons butter or margarine

2 squares **BAKER'S** Unsweetened Baking Chocolate

2 tablespoons cold milk

1 cup sifted powdered sugar

POUR 1¾ cups milk into large bowl. Add dry pudding mix. Beat with wire whisk 2 minutes. Gently stir in whipped topping. Layer one-third of the grahams and half of the whipped topping mixture in 13×9-inch baking pan, breaking grahams as necessary to fit; repeat layers. Top with remaining grahams.

PLACE butter, chocolate and 2 tablespoons milk in small saucepan; cook on low heat until chocolate is completely melted and mixture is blended. Gradually add sugar, stirring until well blended. Spread over grahams.

REFRIGERATE several hours or overnight. Store any leftover dessert in refrigerator.

Makes 24 servings.

"Tastes like an éclair, but oh so easy to make!"
—*Sarah Dicello, Kraft Kitchens*

15 Minute Prep — Lemon-Lime Daiquiri Layered Dessert

Total: 3 hours 25 minutes (includes refrigerating)

- 2 cups lime sherbet, softened
- 1 container (8 ounces) **PHILADELPHIA** Cream Cheese Spread
- 1 can (14 ounces) sweetened condensed milk
- ½ cup lemon juice
- 1 tub (8 ounces) **COOL WHIP** Whipped Topping, thawed

LINE 9×5-inch loaf pan with foil. Spoon sherbet into prepared pan; spread to form even layer in pan. Freeze 10 minutes.

BEAT cream cheese spread in large bowl with wire whisk until creamy. Gradually add sweetened condensed milk and lemon juice, beating until well blended. Stir in whipped topping; spread over sherbet layer in pan.

FREEZE at least 3 hours or overnight. Invert loaf onto a serving plate and remove foil. Garnish with lemon and lime slices, if desired. Cut into 12 slices to serve. Store leftover dessert in freezer.

Makes 12 servings.

Wave-Your-Flag Cake

Total: 20 minutes (includes refrigerating)

1   quart strawberries (4 cups), divided
1½ cups boiling water
1   package (8-serving size) or 2 packages
     (4-serving size each) **JELL-O** Strawberry Flavor Gelatin
     Ice cubes
1   cup cold water
1   package (12 ounces) pound cake, cut into 10 slices
1⅓ cups blueberries, divided
1   tub (8 ounces) **COOL WHIP** Whipped Topping, thawed

SLICE 1 cup of the strawberries. Halve remaining strawberries; set aside.

STIR boiling water into dry gelatin mix in large bowl 2 minutes until completely dissolved. Add enough ice to cold water to measure 2 cups. Add to gelatin; stir until ice is melted. Refrigerate 5 minutes or until slightly thickened (consistency of unbeaten egg whites). Meanwhile, line bottom of 13×9-inch dish with cake slices. Add sliced strawberries and 1 cup of the blueberries to thickened gelatin; stir gently. Spoon over cake slices.

REFRIGERATE 4 hours or until firm. Spread whipped topping over gelatin. Arrange strawberry halves on whipped topping for "stripes" of "flag." Arrange remaining ⅓ cup blueberries on whipped topping for "stars." Store in refrigerator.

Makes 18 servings.

- - - - - - - - - -

WAVE-YOUR-FLAG CHEESECAKE: Prepare cake and gelatin layers as directed. Refrigerate 4 hours or until firm. Beat 2 packages (8 ounces each) softened PHILADELPHIA Cream Cheese and ¼ cup sugar with wire whisk or electric mixer until well blended; gently stir in whipped topping. Spread over gelatin layer. Continue as directed.

JELL-O Mini Trifle Bites

Total: 2 hours 10 minutes (includes refrigerating)

2   cups boiling water

2   packages (4-serving size each) **JELL-O** Raspberry Flavor
     Sugar Free Low Calorie Gelatin

3   slices (¾-inch-thick each) fat free pound cake, cut into
     24 cubes

1   package (8 ounces) **PHILADELPHIA** Neufchâtel Cheese,
     ⅓ Less Fat than Cream Cheese, softened

1   cup powdered sugar

1   cup thawed **COOL WHIP LITE** Whipped Topping

1   teaspoon grated lemon peel

PLACE foil liners in 24 miniature muffin pan cups. Stir boiling water into dry gelatin mixes in large bowl 2 minutes until completely dissolved. Place 1 cake cube in each muffin cup; pour gelatin over cake to fill cup completely. Refrigerate 2 hours or until set.

BEAT cream cheese in small bowl with electric mixer on medium speed until creamy. Gradually add sugar, beating until well blended after each addition. Gently stir in whipped topping and lemon peel until well blended.

FILL pastry bag fitted with star tip with cream cheese mixture. Pipe decorative dollop of cream cheese mixture on top of each trifle.

Makes 12 servings, 2 trifles each.

- - - - - - - - - -

SUBSTITUTE: This recipe can be made with any flavor JELL-O Gelatin.

15 Minute Prep — Triple-Layer Lemon Meringue Pie

Total: 3 hours 15 minutes
(includes refrigerating)

- 2 cups cold milk
- 2 packages (4-serving size each) **JELL-O** Lemon Flavor Instant Pudding & Pie Filling
- 1 tablespoon lemon juice
- 1 **HONEY MAID** Graham Pie Crust (6 ounces)
- 1 tub (8 ounces) **COOL WHIP** Whipped Topping, thawed, divided
- 2½ cups **JET-PUFFED** Miniature Marshmallows, divided
- 2 tablespoons cold milk

POUR 2 cups milk into large bowl. Add dry pudding mixes and juice. Beat with wire whisk 2 minutes or until well blended. (Mixture will be thick.)

SPREAD 1½ cups of the pudding onto bottom of crust; set aside. Add half of the whipped topping to remaining pudding; stir gently until well blended. Spread over pudding layer in crust. Place 2 cups of the marshmallows in large microwaveable bowl. Add 2 tablespoons milk; stir. Microwave on HIGH 1½ minutes or until marshmallows are completely melted, stirring after 1 minute. Stir until well blended. Refrigerate 15 minutes or until cooled. Gently stir in whipped topping; spread over pudding mixture.

REFRIGERATE 3 hours or until set. Top with the remaining ½ cup marshmallows just before serving. Store leftover pie in refrigerator.

Makes 8 servings, 1 slice each.

- - - - - - - - - -

JAZZ IT UP: Garnish with lemon twists or ½ cup sliced strawberries just before serving.

*"Marshmallows are the secret ingredient
in this easy, impressive meringue."*
—*Sarah Dicello, Kraft Kitchens*

Melon Bubbles

Total: 4 hours 45 minutes (includes refrigerating)

1½   cups boiling water
  2   packages (4-serving size each) **JELL-O** Melon Fusion
      Gelatin
2½   cups cold club soda
  ⅓   cup *each*: cantaloupe, honeydew and watermelon balls

STIR boiling water into dry gelatin mix in large bowl at least
2 minutes until completely dissolved. Stir in club soda. Refrigerate
1½ hours or until thickened (spoon drawn through leaves definite
impression).

MEASURE 1 cup thickened gelatin into medium bowl; set aside.
Stir melon balls into remaining gelatin. Spoon into 8 dessert
glasses.

BEAT reserved gelatin with electric mixer on high speed until
fluffy and about doubled in volume. Spoon over gelatin in
glasses. Refrigerate 3 hours or until firm. Store any leftover
desserts in refrigerator.

Makes 8 servings.

-- -- -- -- -- --

SUBSTITUTE: Prepare as directed, using seltzer instead of club soda.

Cool 'n Icy Treats

Fantastic frosty desserts and beverages

OREO Ice Cream Shop Pie

Total: 4 hours 15 minutes (includes freezing)

½ cup hot fudge dessert topping, divided

1 **OREO** Pie Crust (6 ounces)

1 tub (8 ounces) **COOL WHIP** Whipped Topping, thawed, divided

1¼ cups cold milk

2 packages (4-serving size each) **JELL-O OREO** Flavor Instant Pudding & Pie Filling

REMOVE 2 tablespoons of the fudge topping; refrigerate for later use. Spoon remaining topping into crust; spread to evenly cover bottom of crust. Top with half of the whipped topping; freeze 10 minutes.

POUR milk into large bowl. Add dry pudding mixes. Beat with wire whisk 2 minutes or until well blended. (Mixture will be thick.) Gently stir in remaining whipped topping. Spoon over whipped topping layer in crust.

FREEZE 4 hours or until firm. Remove pie from freezer 15 minutes before serving. Let stand at room temperature to soften slightly. Drizzle with the reserved 2 tablespoons fudge topping. Store leftover pie in freezer.

Makes 10 servings.

- - - - - - - - - - -

SUBSTITUTE: Prepare as directed using a HONEY MAID Pie Crust.

Frozen Lemonade Squares

Total: 4 hours 20 minutes (includes freezing)

9 **HONEY MAID** Low Fat Honey Grahams, finely crushed (about 1 ¼ cups crumbs)

⅓ cup margarine or butter, melted

1 quart (4 cups) frozen vanilla yogurt, softened

1 can (6 ounces) frozen lemonade concentrate, thawed

½ cup thawed **COOL WHIP LITE** Whipped Topping

Fresh mint sprigs and lemon slices (optional)

MIX graham crumbs and margarine. Press firmly onto bottom of 9-inch square pan.

BEAT yogurt and lemonade concentrate in large bowl with electric mixer on medium speed until well blended. Spread over crust.

FREEZE 4 hours or until firm. Cut into squares. Top each square with a dollop of whipped topping. Garnish with fresh mint sprigs and lemon slices, if desired.

Makes 9 servings, 1 square each.

- - - - - - - - - -

JAZZ IT UP: Serve this refreshing dessert with fresh raspberries.

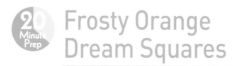

Frosty Orange Dream Squares

Total: 3 hours 20 minutes (includes freezing)

40 **NILLA** Wafers, finely crushed (about 1½ cups)

¼ cup (½ stick) butter, melted

2 cups cold milk

2 packages (4-serving size each) **JELL-O** Vanilla Flavor Instant Pudding & Pie Filling

1 tub (8 ounces) **COOL WHIP** Whipped Topping, thawed, divided

1 pint (2 cups) orange sherbet, softened

LINE 13×9-inch pan with foil, with ends of foil extending over sides of pan. Combine wafer crumbs and butter. Press firmly onto bottom of prepared pan; set aside until ready to use.

ADD milk to dry pudding mixes in medium bowl. Beat with wire whisk 2 minutes or until well blended. Gently stir in half of the whipped topping. Spoon evenly over crust. Refrigerate 10 minutes. Add remaining whipped topping to sherbet; stir with wire whisk until well blended. Spoon evenly over pudding layer; cover.

FREEZE at least 3 hours or overnight. Use foil handles to remove dessert from pan before cutting into squares to serve. Store leftover dessert in freezer.

Makes 24 servings, 1 square each.

SUBSTITUTE: Prepare as directed, using lime or raspberry sherbet.

"This classic flavor combo is sure to bring back memories of a favorite summer dessert."
—*Sarah Dicello, Kraft Kitchens*

No-Melt Sundae Pie

Total: 6 hours 15 minutes (includes freezing)

15 **OREO** Chocolate Sandwich Cookies, crushed (about
    1 ½ cups crumbs)

 3 tablespoons butter, melted

 1 tub (8 ounces) **COOL WHIP** Whipped Topping, thawed,
    divided

 1 cup cold milk

 1 package (4-serving size) **JELL-O** Vanilla Flavor Instant
    Pudding & Pie Filling

 2 squares **BAKER'S** Semi-Sweet Baking Chocolate, melted

 ⅓ cup canned sweetened condensed milk

MIX crumbs and butter; press onto bottom and up side of 9-inch
pie plate. Reserve ½ cup of the whipped topping. Refrigerate
until ready to use.

POUR milk into large bowl. Add dry pudding mix. Beat with
wire whisk 2 minutes or until well blended. Gently stir in
remaining whipped topping. Spoon into crust. Mix melted
chocolate and condensed milk until well blended. Spoon over
pie. Cut through chocolate mixture several times with knife for
marble effect.

FREEZE 6 hours or until firm. Remove pie from freezer 15
minutes before serving. Let stand at room temperature to soften
slightly. Top with the reserved whipped topping.

Makes 10 servings.

Frozen Chocolate Soufflés

Total: 5 hours 10 minutes (includes freezing)

3 cups cold milk

1 package (8-serving size) or 2 packages (4-serving size each) **JELL-O** Chocolate Flavor Instant Pudding & Pie Filling

2 cups thawed **COOL WHIP** Whipped Topping

16 **OREO** Chocolate Sandwich Cookies, chopped (about 2 cups)

8 maraschino cherries

POUR milk into medium bowl. Add dry pudding mix. Beat with wire whisk 2 minutes. Gently stir in whipped topping.

SPOON 2 tablespoons of the chopped cookies into each of 8 (8- to 9-ounce) paper drinking cups. Cover evenly with half of the pudding mixture. Repeat layers. Cover with foil.

FREEZE 5 hours or until firm. Remove from freezer about 15 minutes before serving. Let stand at room temperature to soften slightly. Peel away paper to unmold soufflés onto plates. Top each with a cherry. Store leftover soufflés in freezer.

Makes 8 servings, 1 soufflé each.

VARIATION: Prepare as directed, using JELL-O Vanilla Flavor Instant Pudding & Pie Filling and CHIPS AHOY! Real Chocolate Chip Cookies.

OREO & Fudge Ice Cream Cake

Total: 4 hours 10 minutes (includes freezing)

½ cup hot fudge dessert topping, warmed

1 tub (8 ounces) **COOL WHIP** Whipped Topping, thawed, divided

1 package (4-serving size) **JELL-O** Chocolate Flavor Instant Pudding & Pie Filling

8 **OREO** Chocolate Sandwich Cookies, chopped (about 1 cup)

12 vanilla ice cream sandwiches

POUR fudge topping into medium bowl. Add 1 cup of the whipped topping; stir with wire whisk until well blended. Add dry pudding mix; stir 2 minutes or until well blended. Gently stir in chopped cookies; set aside.

ARRANGE 4 of the ice cream sandwiches, side-by-side, on 24-inch-long piece of foil; top with half of the whipped topping mixture. Repeat layers. Top with remaining 4 ice cream sandwiches. Frost top and sides of dessert with remaining whipped topping. Bring up foil sides. Double fold top and ends to loosely seal packet.

FREEZE at least 4 hours before serving. Store leftover dessert in freezer.

Makes 12 servings.

- - - - - - - - - -

SUBSTITUTE: Prepare as directed, using Neapolitan ice cream sandwiches.

"Sangria" Fruit Cups

Total: 4 hours 20 minutes (includes refrigerating)

1 cup orange juice

1 package (4-serving size) **JELL-O** Strawberry Flavor Gelatin

1 package (4-serving size) **JELL-O** Lemon Flavor Gelatin

1½ cups cold water

1 cup pitted fresh sweet cherries, halved

1 cup quartered strawberries (about 8 medium)

1 cup sliced peeled nectarines (about 1 medium)

1 cup thawed **COOL WHIP** Whipped Topping

BRING orange juice to boil. Add to dry gelatin mixes in medium bowl; stir at least 2 minutes until gelatin is completely dissolved. Stir in cold water.

SPOON fruit evenly into 8 clear cups. Pour gelatin mixture over fruit.

REFRIGERATE 4 hours or until firm. Top with whipped topping just before serving. Store leftover desserts in refrigerator.

Makes 8 servings, about ½ cup each.

- - - - - - - - - - -

SUBSTITUTE: Substitute seedless grape halves for the cherries.

Creamy Carnival Cups

Total: 40 minutes (includes refrigerating)

1   cup boiling water

1   package (4-serving size) **JELL-O** Strawberry Flavor
    Gelatin

2   cups vanilla ice cream

⅓   cup thawed **COOL WHIP** Whipped Topping

STIR boiling water into dry gelatin mix in medium bowl at least
2 minutes until completely dissolved. Stir in ice cream with wire
whisk until well blended.

POUR into 6 dessert bowls. Refrigerate 30 minutes or until set.

TOP each serving with about 1 tablespoon whipped topping just
before serving.

Makes 6 servings, ½ cup each.

- - - - - - - - - -

SUBSTITUTE: Prepare as directed, using JELL-O Lemon Flavor Gelatin.

Frozen Peach Shortcake Squares

10 Minute Prep

Total: 3 hours 10 minutes (includes freezing)

1	tub (8 ounces) **COOL WHIP** Whipped Topping, thawed
1	pint (2 cups) vanilla ice cream, softened
1	package (4-serving size) **JELL-O** Peach Flavor Gelatin
4	cups pound cake cubes
¼	cup raspberry preserves
12	small peach slices
12	raspberries

MIX whipped topping, ice cream and dry gelatin mix in large bowl until well blended. Stir in cake cubes. Spoon into 8-inch square pan.

FREEZE 3 hours or until firm.

DRIZZLE with raspberry preserves. Cut into squares. Top each square with 1 peach slice and 1 raspberry. Store any leftover dessert in freezer.

Makes 12 servings, 1 square each.

Frosty Lemon Ice

Total: 3 hours 20 minutes (includes freezing)

1 cup boiling water
1 package (4-serving size) **JELL-O** Lemon Flavor Sugar Free
   Low Calorie Gelatin
1 cup chilled lemon lime-flavored seltzer
½ teaspoon grated lemon peel
3 tablespoons fresh lemon juice

STIR boiling water into dry gelatin mix in medium bowl at least
2 minutes until completely dissolved. Stir in seltzer, lemon peel
and juice. Pour into 9-inch square pan; cover.

FREEZE 3 hours or until frozen. Let stand at room temperature
10 minutes.

BEAT with electric mixer or blend in covered blender container
on high speed until smooth. Spoon into dessert dishes. Store
leftover ice in freezer.

Makes 6 servings.

JAZZ IT UP: Garnish with fresh lemon slices and mint sprigs.

Rocket Pops

Total: 7 hours 30 minutes (includes freezing)

1 package (4-serving size) **JELL-O** Cherry Flavor Gelatin
1 cup sugar, divided
2 cups boiling water, divided
 Ice cubes
2 cups cold water, divided
1 package (4-serving size) **JELL-O** Berry Blue Flavor Gelatin
1 tub (8 ounces) **COOL WHIP** Whipped Topping, thawed

COMBINE dry cherry gelatin mix and ½ cup of the sugar in medium bowl. Add 1 cup of the boiling water; stir at least 2 minutes until gelatin is completely dissolved. Add enough ice cubes to 1 cup of the cold water to measure 2 cups. Add to gelatin; stir until ice is completely melted. Pour evenly into 16 (5-ounce) paper or plastic cups, adding about ¼ cup of the gelatin to each cup. Freeze 1 hour.

MEANWHILE, combine dry blue gelatin mix and remaining ½ cup sugar in medium bowl. Add remaining 1 cup boiling water; stir at least 2 minutes until gelatin is completely dissolved. Add enough ice cubes to remaining 1 cup cold water to measure 2 cups. Add to gelatin; stir until ice is completely melted. Refrigerate 1 hour.

SPOON about 3 tablespoons of the whipped topping over red gelatin in each cup; top evenly with blue gelatin, adding about ¼ cup of the gelatin to each cup. Freeze 1 hour or until almost firm. Insert wooden pop stick or plastic spoon into center of each cup for handle. Freeze an additional 4 hours or overnight. To remove pops from cups, place bottoms of cups under warm running water for 15 seconds. Press firmly on bottoms of cups to release pops. (Do not twist or pull pop sticks.) Store leftover pops in freezer.

Makes 16 servings.

Mixed Berry Smoothie

Total: 10 minutes

2   cups cold milk

1   container (6 ounces) strawberry low-fat yogurt

1   package (4-serving size) **JELL-O** Strawberry Flavor
     Gelatin

1   cup frozen mixed berries

2   biscuits **POST** Shredded Wheat Cereal, crumbled

PLACE all ingredients in blender; cover.

BLEND on high speed 15 seconds or until smooth.

SERVE immediately.

Makes 4 servings, about 1 cup each.

- - - - - - - - - -

FRESH BANANA PUDDING SMOOTHIE: Prepare as directed, using 3 cups milk, 1 package (4-serving size) JELL-O Vanilla Flavor Instant Pudding and Pie Filling, 2 ripe bananas and 1/2 cup POST SELECTS BANANA NUT CRUNCH Cereal.

PEACHY STRAWBERRY SMOOTHIE: Prepare as directed, using 1 1/2 cups milk, 1 container (6 ounces) plain nonfat yogurt, 1 1/2 teaspoons CRYSTAL LIGHT Raspberry Ice Flavor Low Calorie Soft Drink Mix, 1 cup each frozen sliced peaches and frozen strawberries and 1/2 cup POST HONEY BUNCHES OF OATS Cereal.

Frozen Coolwich

Total: 4 hours 15 minutes (includes freezing)

½ cup hot fudge dessert topping

10 **HONEY MAID** Honey Grahams, broken in half (20 squares)

2 cups thawed **COOL WHIP** Whipped Topping

¼ cup multi-colored sprinkles

SPREAD hot fudge topping evenly onto 10 of the graham squares.

COVER each of the 10 remaining graham squares with about a
¾-inch-thick layer of whipped topping; top each with a fudge-
topped square, fudge side down, to make sandwich. Press together
lightly to secure. Roll or lightly press edges in sprinkles.

FREEZE 4 hours or overnight. Wrap individually with plastic wrap
or foil. Store in freezer up to 2 weeks.

Makes 10 servings.

– – – – – – – – – – –

SUBSTITUTE: Any number of garnishes can be used in place of the
sprinkles, including small candies, finely crushed NABISCO Cookies,
chopped candy bars and toasted BAKER'S ANGEL FLAKE Coconut.

Berry-licious Delights

Delicious desserts using summer fruits

 25 Minute Prep

Summer Berry Pie

Total: 4 hours 30 minutes (includes refrigerating)

- ¾ cup sugar
- 3 tablespoons cornstarch
- 1½ cups water
- 1 package (4-serving size) **JELL-O** Strawberry Flavor Gelatin
- 1 cup each: blueberries, raspberries and sliced strawberries
- 1 **HONEY MAID** Graham Pie Crust (6 ounces)
- 1½ cups thawed **COOL WHIP** Whipped Topping

MIX sugar and cornstarch in medium saucepan. Gradually add water, stirring until well blended. Bring to boil on medium heat, stirring constantly; boil 1 minute. Remove from heat. Add dry gelatin mix; stir until dissolved. Stir in fruit.

POUR into crust.

REFRIGERATE 3 hours or until firm. Top with whipped topping just before serving. Store any leftover pie in refrigerator.

Makes 10 servings.

Fast Fruity Delight

Take ¾ cup boiling water and 1 cup thawed **COOL WHIP** Whipped Topping and mix & match your recipe from these options...

JELL-O Gelatin Flavor options	**frozen fruit** choices
Strawberry	strawberries
Blackberry Fusion (featured in photo)	raspberries
Orange	mixed fruit blend
Berry Blue	blueberries

Just follow our 3 simple steps:

1. Stir boiling water into 1 package (4-serving size) **JELL-O Gelatin** in large bowl at least 2 minutes until completely dissolved.

2. Add 2 cups **frozen fruit**; stir until gelatin starts to thicken. Mix ½ cup of the gelatin mixture into whipped topping with wire whisk until well blended.

3. Spoon whipped topping mixture evenly into 4 dessert cups. Spoon remaining gelatin and fruit mixture over whipped topping mixture in each cup. Refrigerate 15 minutes or until set. Store any leftover dessert cups in refrigerator.

Makes 4 servings.

- - - - - - - - - -

MAKE IT EASY: The frozen fruit makes setting the gelatin quick and easy.

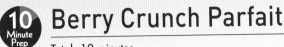 # Berry Crunch Parfait

Total: 10 minutes

½   cup sliced strawberries

2   tablespoons thawed **COOL WHIP LITE** Whipped Topping

2   tablespoons **POST HONEY BUNCHES OF OATS** Cereal

PLACE half of the strawberries in 8-ounce glass; top with layers of 1 tablespoon each of the whipped topping and cereal.

COVER with layers of the remaining strawberries and cereal

TOP with the remaining whipped topping.

Makes 1 serving.

- - - - - - - - - -

SUBSTITUTE: Prepare as directed, substituting your favorite summer berries for the sliced strawberries.

Mixed Berry Freezer Jam

Total: 30 minutes plus standing

1   quart strawberries, stemmed, mashed

1   pint raspberries, mashed

1   pint blueberries, mashed

3   cups sugar

1   box **SURE-JELL** For Less or No Sugar Needed Recipes
    Premium Fruit Pectin

1   cup water

MEASURE 2 cups mashed strawberries and 1 cup each mashed raspberries and blueberries into large bowl; mix well.

BRING sugar, pectin and water to a boil in large saucepan, stirring constantly. Boil and stir 1 minute. Remove from heat.

ADD fruit mixture; stir 1 minute or until thoroughly mixed.

FILL clean plastic containers immediately to within ½-inch of tops; cover with lids. Let stand at room temperature for 24 hours until set. Store in refrigerator up to 3 weeks or freeze extra containers up to 1 year. Thaw in refrigerator before using.

Makes about 7 (1-cup) containers, or 112 servings, 1 tablespoon each.

– – – – – – – – – –

NOTE: This jam is the essence of summer. It's so good, you'll want to keep some in the freezer for year-round enjoyment.

ⓕ PHILADELPHIA "Fruit Smoothie" No-Bake Cheesecake

Total: 4 hours 15 minutes (includes refrigerating)

1½ cups **HONEY MAID** Graham Cracker Crumbs

¼ cup (½ stick) butter, melted

2 tablespoons sugar

4 packages (8 ounces each) **PHILADELPHIA** Neufchâtel Cheese, ⅓ Less Fat than Cream Cheese, softened

½ cup sugar

1 package (12 ounces) frozen mixed berries (strawberries, raspberries, blueberries and blackberries), thawed, drained

1 tub (8 ounces) **COOL WHIP LITE** Whipped Topping, thawed

LINE 13×9-inch baking pan with foil, with ends of foil extending over sides of pan. Mix graham crumbs, butter and 2 tablespoons sugar; press firmly onto bottom of prepared pan. Refrigerate while preparing filling.

BEAT Neufchâtel cheese and ½ cup sugar in large bowl with electric mixer on medium speed until well blended. Smash drained berries with fork; stir into Neufchâtel cheese mixture. Gently stir in whipped topping. Spoon over crust; cover.

REFRIGERATE 4 hours or until firm. Use foil handles to remove cheesecake from pan before cutting into pieces to serve. Store leftover cheesecake in refrigerator.

Makes 16 servings, 1 piece each.

- - - - - - - - - -

SUBSTITUTE: Prepare as directed, substituting 3 cups fresh mixed berries for the 12-ounce package of frozen mixed berries and increasing the sugar in the Neufchâtel cheese mixture from ½ cup to ¾ cup.

Cherry Celebration

Total: 4 hours 30 minutes

- 2 cups boiling water
- 2 packages (4-serving size each) **JELL-O** Cherry Flavor Gelatin
- 4 cups ice cubes
- 3 cups thawed **COOL WHIP** Whipped Topping
- 1 cup cherry pie filling

STIR boiling water into dry gelatin mix in large bowl until completely dissolved. Add ice cubes; stir until gelatin begins to thicken. Remove any unmelted ice.

ADD whipped topping; stir with wire whisk until well blended. Refrigerate until slightly thickened, about 20 minutes.

ADD cherry pie filling; stir gently until well blended. Spoon into 12 champagne glasses or a glass bowl. Refrigerate 4 hours or overnight. Garnish with additional whipped topping and cherry pie filling just before serving, if desired.

Makes 12 servings, ⅔ cup each.

- - - - - - - - - -

JAZZ IT UP: For an extra special touch, use a spoon to drizzle melted BAKER'S Baking Chocolate on inside of empty serving bowl. Refrigerate several hours or overnight. Fill with pie filling mixture and refrigerate as directed.

Berry Squares

Total: 1 hour 15 minutes (includes refrigerating)

1   package (12 ounces) pound cake, cut into 10 slices

3   tablespoons orange juice

2   pints fresh berries (strawberries, raspberries and/or blueberries)

2   tablespoons sugar

2½ cups cold milk

2   packages (4-serving size each) **JELL-O** French Vanilla Flavor Instant Pudding & Pie Filling

1   tub (8 ounces) **COOL WHIP** Whipped Topping, thawed, divided

ARRANGE cake slices on bottom of 13×9-inch dish, cutting to fit if necessary; drizzle with juice. Top with berries; sprinkle with sugar.

POUR milk into large bowl. Add dry pudding mixes. Beat with wire whisk 2 minutes. Gently stir in 1 cup of the whipped topping; spread over berries. Top with remaining whipped topping.

REFRIGERATE at least 1 hour before cutting into squares to serve.

Makes 15 servings, 1 square each.

- - - - - - - - - -

HEALTHY LIVING: For a low-fat version of this luscious dessert, prepare with fat free pound cake, fat free milk, JELL-O Vanilla Flavor Fat Free Sugar Free Instant Reduced Calorie Pudding & Pie Filling and COOL WHIP FREE Whipped Topping. It has 80 fewer calories and 80% less fat per serving.

JELL-O Magic Mousse

Total: 8 hours 10 minutes (includes refrigerating)

1½ cups boiling water

1 package (4-serving size) **JELL-O** Strawberry Flavor
   Gelatin

1 tub (8 ounces) **COOL WHIP** Whipped Topping, thawed

1 cup fresh berries (sliced strawberries, blueberries and
   raspberries)

STIR boiling water into dry gelatin mix in medium bowl at least
2 minutes until completely dissolved. Add whipped topping; stir
with wire whisk until whipped topping is completely melted and
mixture is well blended. (Mixture will be thin.)

FILL dessert cups evenly with gelatin mixture.

REFRIGERATE at least 2 hours or until layers separate. Top with
fruit. Store leftover desserts in refrigerator.

Makes 5 servings, about ½ cup each.

- - - - - - - - - -

SHORTCUT: Is the whipped topping still frozen? No need to worry. Just
follow the recipe as directed, using the still-frozen whipped topping.
Just be sure to stir the gelatin mixture until the whipped topping is
completely melted as directed before pouring into the prepared
mold.

"The frozen whipped topping melts into the gelatin causing it to magically separate into two layers."
—*Sarah Dicello, Kraft Kitchens*

Sparkling Berry Dessert

Total: 4 hours 40 minutes (includes refrigerating)

1½   cups boiling water
1   package (8-serving size) **JELL-O** Raspberry Flavor Gelatin
2½   cups cold club soda
1   cup sliced strawberries

STIR boiling water into dry gelatin mix in large bowl at least
2 minutes until completely dissolved. Add club soda; stir.
Refrigerate 1½ hours or until thickened (spoon drawn through
leaves definite impression).

REMOVE 1 cup of the thickened gelatin; place in medium bowl.
Set aside. Stir strawberries into remaining gelatin. Spoon evenly
into 8 champagne glasses or dessert dishes.

BEAT reserved 1 cup gelatin with electric mixer on high speed
until fluffy and about doubled in volume. Spoon over gelatin in
glasses; cover. Refrigerate 3 hours or until firm. Store any leftover
desserts in refrigerator.

Makes 8 servings.

- - - - - - - - - -

SUBSTITUTE: Prepare as directed, using seltzer instead of club soda.

 # Triple Berry Parfaits

Total: 15 minutes

⅔   cup *each*: raspberries, sliced strawberries and blueberries

3   containers (6 ounces each) strawberry nonfat yogurt

¼   cup **BAKER'S ANGEL FLAKE** Coconut

24   Reduced Fat **NILLA** Wafers, coarsely chopped

6   tablespoons thawed **COOL WHIP LITE** Whipped Topping

MIX fruit in medium bowl. Add yogurt and coconut; toss to coat.

SPOON half of the chopped wafers evenly into 6 parfait glasses; cover with half of the fruit mixture. Repeat layers.

TOP with the whipped topping.

Makes 6 servings.

- - - - - - - - - -

MAKE AHEAD: Prepare parfaits as directed. Cover and refrigerate up to 1 hour before serving.

Strawberry Dessert Pizza

Total: 40 minutes

1 package (20 ounces) refrigerated sugar cookie dough

1 package (8 ounces) **PHILADELPHIA** Cream Cheese, softened

⅓ cup sugar

1 tub (8 ounces) **COOL WHIP** Strawberry Whipped Topping, thawed

1 pint (2 cups) strawberries, sliced

PREHEAT oven to 350°F. Press dough firmly into greased 12-inch pizza pan. Bake 20 minutes or until golden brown. Cool in pan on wire rack.

BEAT cream cheese and sugar in large bowl with wire whisk or electric mixer on high speed until well blended. Gently stir in whipped topping.

SPREAD cream cheese mixture over crust; top with strawberries. Serve immediately. Or cover and refrigerate until ready to serve. Store any leftover dessert in refrigerator.

Makes 12 servings.

- - - - - - - - - -

SUBSTITUTE: Prepare as directed, using regular COOL WHIP Whipped Topping.

"Easy as pie to make! I also like using raspberries and blueberries with the strawberries."
—*Sarah Dicello, Kraft Kitchens*

45 SURE-JELL
Strawberry Jam

Total: 45 minutes

5 cups prepared fruit (about 2 quarts fully ripe strawberries)
1 box **SURE-JELL** Fruit Pectin
½ teaspoon butter or margarine (optional)
7 cups sugar, measured into separate bowl

BRING boiling-water canner, half full with water, to simmer.
Wash jars and screw bands in hot soapy water; rinse with warm
water. Pour boiling water over flat lids in saucepan off the heat.
Let stand in hot water until ready to use. Drain well before filling.

STEM and crush strawberries thoroughly, 1 layer at a time.
Measure exactly 5 cups prepared fruit into 6- or 8-quart
saucepot.

STIR pectin into prepared fruit in saucepot. Add butter to reduce
foaming, if desired. Bring mixture to full rolling boil (a boil
that doesn't stop bubbling when stirred) on high heat, stirring
constantly. Stir in sugar. Return to full rolling boil and boil exactly
1 minute, stirring constantly. Remove from heat. Skim off any
foam with metal spoon.

LADLE immediately into prepared jars, filling to within ⅛-inch of
tops. Wipe jar rims and threads. Cover with 2-piece lids. Screw
bands tightly. Place jars on elevated rack in canner. Lower
rack into canner. (Water must cover jars by 1 to 2 inches. Add
boiling water, if necessary.) Cover; bring water to gentle boil.
Process 10 minutes. Remove jars and place upright on a towel to
cool completely. After jars cool, check seals by pressing middles
of lids with finger. (If lids spring back, lids are not sealed and
refrigeration is necessary.)

Makes about 8 (1-cup) jars or 128 servings, 1 tablespoon each.

- - - - - - - - - -

HOW TO MEASURE PRECISELY: To get exact level cup measures of sugar,
spoon sugar into dry metal or plastic measuring cups, then level by
scraping excess sugar from top of cup with a straight-edged knife.

Strawberry-Swirl Cake

Total: 1 hour 35 minutes (includes cooling)

- 1 package (2-layer size) white cake mix
- 1 package (4-serving size) **JELL-O** Strawberry Flavor Gelatin
- ⅔ cup **BREAKSTONE'S** or **KNUDSEN** Sour Cream
- ⅔ cup powdered sugar
- 1 tub (8 ounces) **COOL WHIP** Whipped Topping, thawed
- 1 cup sliced strawberries, plus 2 whole strawberries for garnish

PREHEAT oven to 350°F. Grease 2 (8- or 9-inch) round cake pans; set aside. Prepare cake batter as directed on package. Pour half of the batter into medium bowl. Add dry gelatin mix; stir until well blended. Spoon half of the white batter and half of the pink batter, side by side, into each prepared pan. Lightly swirl batters together using a teaspoon. (Do not overswirl, or the color of the cake will be all pink and not pink and white marbled.)

BAKE 30 minutes. Cool 30 minutes in pans. Remove to wire racks; cool completely.

MIX sour cream and powdered sugar in medium bowl until well blended. Gently stir in whipped topping. Place 1 of the cake layers on serving plate; spread top with 1 cup of the whipped topping mixture. Top with 1 cup of the strawberries and remaining cake layer. Spread top and sides of cake with remaining whipped topping mixture. Garnish with whole strawberries just before serving. Store leftover cake in refrigerator.

Makes 16 servings, 1 slice each.

- - - - - - - - - -

HOW TO PREVENT AIR BUBBLES: To release any air bubbles from the cake batter, lightly tap cake pans on counter before baking. Any small air bubbles will rise to the surface.

"Try using other flavors of gelatin to make your own favorite flavor swirl."
—*Sarah Dicello, Kraft Kitchens*

 # NILLA Nibbles

Total: 5 minutes

4   Reduced Fat **NILLA** Wafers
2   tablespoons thawed **COOL WHIP LITE** Whipped Topping
2   medium strawberries, halved

TOP each wafer with 1½ teaspoons of the whipped topping and 1 strawberry half.

SERVE immediately.

Makes 1 serving.

SUBSTITUTE: Prepare as directed, using COOL WHIP FREE Whipped Topping.

Sensational treats for Healthy Living

Mimosa Mold

Total: 5 hours (includes refrigerating)

1½ cups boiling water

1 package (8-serving size) **JELL-O** Orange Flavor Sugar Free Low Calorie Gelatin

2 cups cold club soda

1 can (11 ounces) mandarin orange segments, drained

1 cup sliced strawberries

STIR boiling water into dry gelatin mix in large bowl at least 2 minutes until completely dissolved. Stir in club soda. Refrigerate 1½ hours or until thickened (spoon drawn through leaves definite impression).

STIR in oranges and strawberries. Pour into 6-cup mold sprayed with cooking spray.

REFRIGERATE 4 hours or until firm. Unmold. Store any leftover gelatin in refrigerator.

Makes 12 servings.

CALORIES 15, CARB 3g, TOTAL FAT 0g (0g SAT. FAT), FIBER 0g, PROTEIN 1g

Very Berry Fruit Cups

Total: 2 hours 15 minutes (includes refrigerating)

¾ cup boiling water

1 package (4-serving size) **JELL-O** Strawberry-Banana Flavor Sugar Free Low Calorie Gelatin

Ice cubes

½ cup cold water

1 cup puréed strawberries

¾ cup thawed **COOL WHIP** Sugar Free Whipped Topping

STIR boiling water into dry gelatin mix in medium bowl at least 2 minutes until completely dissolved. Add enough ice cubes to cold water to measure 1¼ cups. Add to gelatin; stir until slightly thickened. Remove any unmelted ice. Refrigerate 10 minutes or until slightly thickened (consistency of unbeaten egg whites).

ADD strawberries; stir. Pour evenly into 6 dessert dishes.

REFRIGERATE 2 hours or until firm. Store leftover desserts in refrigerator. Dollop each dessert with whipped topping before serving.

Makes 6 servings.

CALORIES 90, CARB 19g, TOTAL FAT 1.5g (1g SAT. FAT), LESS THAN 1g FIBER, PROTEIN 1g

JELL-O Strawberry Mousse Cups

15 Minute Prep

Total: 2 hours 15 minutes (includes refrigerating)

¾ cup boiling water

1 package (4-serving size) **JELL-O** Strawberry Flavor Sugar Free Low Calorie Gelatin

1 cup ice cubes

2 cups thawed **COOL WHIP** Sugar Free Whipped Topping, divided

1 pint strawberries, sliced (about 2 cups), divided

STIR boiling water into dry gelatin mix in large bowl at least 2 minutes until completely dissolved. Add ice cubes; stir until completely melted. Gently stir in 1½ cups each of the whipped topping and strawberries until well blended.

SPOON evenly into 6 small dessert dishes. Refrigerate 2 hours or until firm.

TOP with the remaining ½ cup whipped topping and remaining strawberries just before serving. Store any leftover dessert cups in refrigerator.

Makes 6 servings, 1 dessert cup each.

CALORIES 80, CARB 11g, TOTAL FAT 3.5g (1.5g SAT. FAT), FIBER 1g, PROTEIN 1g

Low-Fat Chocolate-Banana Parfaits

Total: 10 minutes

2 cups cold fat free milk

1 package (4-serving size) **JELL-O** Chocolate Flavor Fat Free Sugar Free Instant Reduced Calorie Pudding & Pie Filling

2 medium bananas, sliced

¾ cup thawed **COOL WHIP** Sugar Free Whipped Topping, divided

POUR milk into medium bowl. Add dry pudding mix. Beat with wire whisk 2 minutes or until well blended.

SPOON half of the pudding evenly into 4 dessert glasses. Cover with layers of banana slices, ½ cup of the whipped topping and the remaining pudding. Top with remaining whipped topping.

SERVE immediately. Or cover and refrigerate until ready to serve.

Makes 4 servings, 1 parfait each.

CALORIES 160, CARB 33g, TOTAL FAT 2g (2g SAT. FAT), FIBER 3g, PROTEIN 5g

Delightful Lemon Mousse with Raspberry Sauce

Total: 4 hours 15 minutes (includes refrigerating)

1½ cups boiling water

1 package (8-serving size) **JELL-O** Lemon Flavor Sugar Free Low Calorie Gelatin

2 teaspoons grated lemon peel

Ice cubes

1 cup cold apple juice

1 tub (8 ounces) **COOL WHIP** Sugar Free Whipped Topping, thawed

1 package (10 ounces) frozen raspberries, thawed, puréed in blender

STIR boiling water into dry gelatin mix and lemon peel in large bowl at least 2 minutes until gelatin is completely dissolved. Add enough ice to apple juice to measure 1¾ cups. Stir into gelatin until slightly thickened. Stir in whipped topping with wire whisk until well blended.

POUR half of the raspberry sauce into 10 dessert dishes. Top with gelatin mixture and remaining raspberry sauce.

REFRIGERATE 4 hours or until firm. Store any leftover dessert in refrigerator. Garnish with fresh raspberries, if desired.

Makes 10 servings.

CALORIES 80, CARB 15g, TOTAL FAT 1.5g (1g SAT. FAT), FIBER 2g, PROTEIN 2g

Angel Lush with Pineapple

Total: 1 hour 15 minutes (includes refrigerating)

1   package (4-serving size) **JELL-O** Vanilla Flavor Instant Pudding & Pie Filling

1   can (20 ounces) **DOLE** Crushed Pineapple in Juice, undrained

1   cup thawed **COOL WHIP** Whipped Topping

1   package (10 ounces) round angel food cake

1   cup fresh mixed berries

MIX dry pudding mix and pineapple with its juice in medium bowl. Gently stir in whipped topping. Let stand 5 minutes until thickened.

CUT cake horizontally into three layers. Place bottom cake layer, cut-side up, on serving plate; top with 1 ⅓ cups of the pudding mixture. Cover with middle cake layer and additional 1 cup of the remaining pudding mixture. Top with remaining cake layer; spread top with the remaining pudding mixture.

REFRIGERATE at least 1 hour. Top with fresh berries just before serving. Store leftover dessert in refrigerator.

Makes 10 servings.

CALORIES 140, CARB 31g, TOTAL FAT 1g (1g SAT. FAT), FIBER 1g, PROTEIN 2g

15 Minute Prep Low-Fat Strawberry Shortcut

Total: 15 minutes

1½ quarts (6 cups) strawberries, sliced

¼ cup sugar

1 package (13.6 ounces) fat free pound cake, cut into 12 slices

1 tub (8 ounces) **COOL WHIP** Sugar Free Whipped Topping, thawed

TOSS strawberries with sugar; let stand 10 minutes or until sugar is dissolved.

CUT each slice of pound cake in half horizontally. Place 1 cake piece on each of 12 dessert plates.

SPOON about ¼ cup of the strawberries over each cake piece; top with 2 tablespoons of the whipped topping. Repeat layers. Serve immediately.

Makes 12 servings.

CALORIES 170, CARB 36g, TOTAL FAT 1.5g (1g SAT. FAT), FIBER 2g, PROTEIN 2g

Frozen Raspberry Shortcake Squares

10 Minute Prep

Total: 3 hours 10 minutes (includes freezing

- 1 pint (2 cups) frozen raspberry nonfat yogurt, softened
- 1 package (4-serving size) **JELL-O** Raspberry Flavor Sugar Free Low Calorie Gelatin
- 1 tub (8 ounces) **COOL WHIP** Sugar Free Whipped Topping, thawed
- 1 package (10.75 ounces) reduced-fat pound cake, cubed

BEAT yogurt and dry gelatin mix in large bowl with wire whisk until well blended. Gently stir in whipped topping. Add cake cubes; mix lightly.

SPOON into 8-inch square pan.

FREEZE 3 hours or until firm. Cut into 12 squares to serve. Store leftover dessert in freezer.

Makes 12 servings, 1 square each.

- - - - - - - - - - -

HOW TO THAW COOL WHIP: Place unopened 8-ounce tub in refrigerator for 4 hours. Do not thaw in microwave.

CALORIES 180, CARB 27g, TOTAL FAT 6g (3.5g SAT. FAT), FIBER 0g, PROTEIN 3g

CONTENTS

152

130

155

176

A TASTE OF HEAVEN

PHILADELPHIA CREAM CHEESE
TIPS FOR THE PERFECT CHEESECAKE

For best quality and results, always use **PHILADELPHIA** Cream Cheese.

Preheating the oven: The baking time indicated in a recipe is based on using a preheated oven. Turn the oven on when you start to mix the cheesecake ingredients. This should allow enough time for the oven to heat to the correct temperature for when you are ready to place the cheesecake in the oven to bake. Unless otherwise indicated, always bake cheesecakes in the center of the middle oven rack.

Beating the batter: While adding ingredients, do not overbeat the cheesecake batter. Too much air beaten into the batter will result in a cheesecake that sinks in the center when cooled.

Baking cheesecakes: Overbaked cheesecakes tend to crack. Remove the cheesecake from the oven when the center is almost set (i.e. center of cheesecake still wiggles when the pan is gently shaken from side-to-side). Although the cheesecake appears underbaked, the residual heat in the cheesecake will be enough to finish baking the center. After chilling, the cheesecake will have a perfectly smooth consistency.

Cooling cheesecakes: Cool cheesecakes completely before refrigerating. Placing a warm cheesecake in the refrigerator will cause condensation to form on the cake, resulting in a soggy cheesecake.

tips for the perfect cheesecake

HOW TO BAKE IN A SPRINGFORM PAN: Preheat oven to 325°F if using a silver 9-inch springform pan (or to 300°F if using a dark nonstick 9-inch springform pan). Prepare crust as directed; press firmly onto bottom of pan. Prepare filling as directed; pour over crust. Bake 1 hour or until center is almost set. Run small knife or small spatula around rim of pan to loosen cake; cool before removing rim of pan. Refrigerate 4 hours or overnight.

New York-Style Sour Cream-Topped Cheesecake *(page 152)*

Cutting cheesecakes: Cut cheesecakes when they are cold rather than warm. Use a sharp knife with a clean, thin blade. To make clean cuts, dip the knife in hot water after each cut and wipe the blade clean.

For all of your occasions, *PHILLY* MAKES A BETTER CHEESECAKE.

During tests of plain New York-style cheesecake made with ***PHILADELPHIA*** *Cream Cheese versus store-brand versions, consumers rated PHILLY cheesecake as better tasting.*

tips for the perfect cheesecake

95

FRESH FRUIT CHEESECAKES

CHEESECAKES PAIRED WITH THE FRESH FRUITS AND FLAVORS OF SUMMER

Lemon Cheesecake

Prep: 15 minutes plus refrigerating ● Bake: 50 minutes

1½ cups **HONEY MAID** Graham Cracker Crumbs

⅓ cup sugar

⅓ cup butter or margarine, melted

3 packages (8 ounces each) **PHILADELPHIA** Cream Cheese, softened

1 cup sugar

1 cup **BREAKSTONE'S** or **KNUDSEN** Sour Cream

3 eggs

   Grated peel and juice from 1 lemon

PREHEAT oven to 325°F if using a silver 9-inch springform pan (or to 300°F if using a dark nonstick 9-inch springform pan). Mix graham crumbs, ⅓ cup sugar and butter. Reserve ½ cup crumb mixture; press remaining crumb mixture firmly onto bottom of pan. Set aside.

BEAT cream cheese and 1 cup sugar in large bowl with electric mixer on medium speed until well blended. Add sour cream; mix well. Add eggs, 1 at a time, mixing on low speed after each addition just until blended. Stir in lemon peel and juice. Pour over crust; sprinkle with reserved crumb mixture.

BAKE 45 to 50 minutes or until center is almost set. Run knife or metal spatula around rim of pan to loosen cake; cool before removing rim. Refrigerate at least 4 hours or overnight. Store leftover cheesecake in refrigerator.

Makes 12 servings.

HOW TO SOFTEN CREAM CHEESE:

Place unwrapped package of cream cheese in microwaveable bowl. Microwave on HIGH (100%) 15 seconds or just until softened. Add 15 seconds for each additional package of cream cheese.

SIZE-WISE:

Looking for a special dessert? Enjoy 1 serving of this elegant lemon cheesecake.

Triple Citrus Cheesecake

Prep: 30 minutes plus refrigerating • Bake: 1 hour 5 minutes

- **1 cup HONEY MAID Graham Cracker Crumbs**
- **⅓ cup firmly packed brown sugar**
- **¼ cup (½ stick) butter or margarine, melted**
- **4 packages (8 ounces each) PHILADELPHIA Cream Cheese, softened**
- **1 cup granulated sugar**
- **2 tablespoons flour**
- **1 teaspoon vanilla**
- **4 eggs**
- **1 tablespoon fresh lemon juice**
- **1 tablespoon fresh lime juice**
- **1 tablespoon fresh orange juice**
- **1 teaspoon grated lemon peel**
- **1 teaspoon grated lime peel**
- **1 teaspoon grated orange peel**

PREHEAT oven to 325°F if using a silver 9-inch springform pan (or to 300°F if using a dark nonstick 9-inch springform pan). Mix crumbs, brown sugar and butter; press firmly onto bottom of pan. Bake 10 minutes.

BEAT cream cheese, granulated sugar, flour and vanilla with electric mixer on medium speed until well blended. Add eggs, 1 at a time, mixing on low speed after each addition just until blended. Stir in remaining ingredients; pour over crust.

BAKE 1 hour and 5 minutes or until center is almost set. Run knife or metal spatula around rim of pan to loosen cake; cool before removing rim of pan. Refrigerate 4 hours or overnight. Store leftover cheesecake in refrigerator.

Makes 16 servings.

Fruit Pizza

Prep: 25 minutes plus refrigerating

1 package (20 ounces) refrigerated sliceable sugar cookies, sliced

1 package (8 ounces) **PHILADELPHIA** Cream Cheese, softened

¼ cup sugar

½ teaspoon vanilla

Assorted fruit, such as sliced kiwi, strawberries, blueberries and drained, canned mandarin orange segments

¼ cup apricot preserves, pressed through sieve to remove lumps

1 tablespoon water

PREHEAT oven to 375°F. Line 12-inch pizza pan with foil; spray with cooking spray. Arrange cookie dough slices in single layer in prepared pan; press together to form crust. Bake 14 minutes; cool. Invert onto serving plate; carefully remove foil. Invert onto large serving plate or tray so crust is right-side-up.

BEAT cream cheese, sugar and vanilla with electric mixer on medium speed until well blended. Spread over crust.

ARRANGE fruit over cream cheese layer. Mix preserves and water; brush over fruit. Refrigerate 2 hours. Cut into 12 wedges to serve. Store leftover dessert in refrigerator.

Makes 12 servings, 1 wedge each.

fresh fruit cheesecakes

Blueberry Swirl Cheesecake

Prep: 15 minutes plus refrigerating ● Bake: 45 minutes

1 cup **HONEY MAID** Graham Cracker Crumbs

1 cup plus 3 tablespoons sugar, divided

3 tablespoons butter or margarine, melted

4 packages (8 ounces each) **PHILADELPHIA** Cream Cheese, softened

1 teaspoon vanilla

1 cup **BREAKSTONE'S** or **KNUDSEN** Sour Cream

4 eggs

2 cups fresh or thawed frozen blueberries

PREHEAT oven to 325°F. Mix crumbs, 3 tablespoons of the sugar and butter. Press firmly onto bottom of foil-lined 13×9-inch baking pan. Bake 10 minutes.

BEAT cream cheese, remaining 1 cup sugar and vanilla in large bowl with electric mixer on medium speed until well blended. Add sour cream; mix well. Add eggs, 1 at a time, beating on low speed after each addition just until blended. Pour over crust. Purée blueberries in a blender or food processor. Gently drop spoonfuls of puréed blueberries over batter; cut through batter several times with knife for marble effect.

BAKE 45 minutes or until center is almost set; cool. Cover and refrigerate at least 4 hours before serving. Store leftover cheesecake in refrigerator.

Makes 16 servings.

SUBSTITUTE:

Substitute 1 can (15 ounces) blueberries, well drained, for the 2 cups fresh or frozen blueberries.

MAKE IT EASY:

Instead of using a blender, crush the blueberries in a bowl with a fork. Drain before spooning over the cheesecake batter and swirling to marbleize as directed.

fresh fruit cheesecakes

EASY & ELEGENT DESSERTS

SIMPLE, SENSATIONAL TREATS

OREO No-Bake Cheesecake

Prep: 15 minutes plus refrigerating

1 package (1 pound 2 ounces) **OREO** Chocolate Sandwich Cookies, divided

¼ cup (½ stick) butter, melted

4 packages (8 ounces each) **PHILADELPHIA** Cream Cheese, softened

½ cup sugar

1 teaspoon vanilla

1 tub (8 ounces) **COOL WHIP** Whipped Topping, thawed

LINE 13×9-inch pan with foil, with ends of foil extending over sides of pan. Coarsely chop 15 of the cookies; set aside. Finely crush remaining cookies; mix with butter. Press firmly onto bottom of prepared pan. Refrigerate while preparing filling.

BEAT cream cheese, sugar and vanilla in large bowl with electric mixer on medium speed until well blended. Gently stir in whipped topping and chopped cookies. Spoon over crust; cover.

REFRIGERATE 4 hours or until firm. Store leftover cheesecake in refrigerator.

Makes 16 servings, 1 piece each.

VARIATION:

Prepare as directed, using 1 package (1 pound 2 ounces) Golden OREO Chocolate Creme Sandwich Cookies or 1 package (17 ounces) OREO DOUBLE STUF Cool Mint Creme Sandwich Cookies.

Key Lime Cheesecake Pie

Prep: 25 minutes plus refrigerating

1¼ cups finely crushed coconut bar cookies

¼ cup (½ stick) butter or margarine, melted

3 tablespoons sugar

2 packages (8 ounces each) **PHILADELPHIA** Cream Cheese, softened

1 can (14 ounces) sweetened condensed milk

½ teaspoon grated lime peel

⅓ cup lime juice

Few drops green food coloring (optional)

PREHEAT oven to 350°F. Mix crumbs, butter and sugar; press firmly onto bottom and up side of 9-inch pie plate. Bake 10 minutes. Cool.

BEAT cream cheese and sweetened condensed milk in large bowl with electric mixer on medium speed until well blended. Add peel, juice and food coloring; mix well. Pour into crust.

REFRIGERATE at least 8 hours or overnight. Store leftover pie in refrigerator.

Makes 10 servings.

HOW TO SOFTEN CREAM CHEESE:

Place unwrapped package of cream cheese in microwaveable bowl. Microwave on HIGH (100%) 15 seconds or just until softened. Add 15 seconds for each additional package of cream cheese.

easy & elegant desserts

Fluffy Cheesecake

Prep: 15 minutes plus refrigerating

1 package (8 ounces) **PHILADELPHIA** Cream Cheese, softened

⅓ cup sugar

1 tub (8 ounces) **COOL WHIP** Whipped Topping, thawed

1 **HONEY MAID** Graham Pie Crust (6 ounces)

1 apple, cored, thinly sliced (optional)

BEAT cream cheese and sugar in large bowl with wire whisk or electric mixer until well blended. Gently stir in whipped topping.

SPOON into crust.

REFRIGERATE 3 hours or until set. Top with apple slices just before serving.

Makes 8 servings.

FLUFFY CHEESECAKE SQUARES:

Omit pie crust. Mix 1 cup HONEY MAID Graham Cracker Crumbs, 2 tablespoons sugar and ⅓ cup melted butter or margarine. Press onto bottom of foil-lined 8-inch square baking pan. Continue as directed. Makes 9 servings.

FLUFFY CHERRY CHEESECAKE:

Omit apple. Prepare and refrigerate as directed. Top with 1½ cups cherry pie filling just before serving.

Cream Cheese Frosting

Prep: 10 minutes

- 1 package (8 ounces) **PHILADELPHIA** Cream Cheese, softened
- ¼ cup (½ stick) butter or margarine, softened
- 1 teaspoon vanilla
- 1 package (16 ounces) powdered sugar (about 4 cups), sifted

BEAT cream cheese, butter and vanilla in large bowl with electric mixer on medium speed until well blended.

ADD sugar gradually, beating until well blended after each addition.

Makes about 2½ cups or 20 servings, 2 tablespoons each.

NOTE:

Recipe makes enough to fill and frost 2 (8- or 9-inch) cake layers or top and sides of 13×9-inch cake or tops of 24 cupcakes.

COOKING KNOW-HOW:

Sift the powdered sugar before adding to the cream cheese mixture for a smoother frosting.

Summer Berry Trifle

Prep: 40 minutes plus refrigerating

- **1** cup boiling water
- **1** package (8-serving size) **JELL-O** Brand Strawberry Flavor Gelatin
  Ice cubes
- **½** cup cold water
- **2** cups mixed berries (raspberries, blueberries, strawberries)
- **1** package (8 ounces) **PHILADELPHIA** Cream Cheese, softened
- **1¼** cups cold milk, divided
- **1** package (4-serving size) **JELL-O** Cheesecake or Vanilla Flavor Instant Pudding & Pie Filling
- **1** tub (8 ounces) **COOL WHIP** Strawberry Whipped Topping, thawed
- **1** package (10.75 ounces) pound cake, cubed

STIR boiling water into dry gelatin in large bowl at least 2 minutes until completely dissolved. Add enough ice to cold water to measure 1 cup. Add to gelatin; stir until ice is completely melted. Let stand about 15 minutes or until thickened. (Spoon drawn through gelatin leaves definite impression.) Stir in berries.

PLACE cream cheese in large bowl; beat with wire whisk until creamy. Gradually add ¼ cup of the milk, beating until well blended. Add remaining 1 cup milk and dry pudding mix; beat 2 minutes or until well blended. Gently stir in whipped topping. Set aside.

PLACE about half of the cake cubes in bottom of large serving bowl; cover with half of the pudding mixture. Top with layers of the gelatin mixture, remaining cake cubes and remaining pudding mixture. Refrigerate at least 1 hour or until ready to serve. Store leftover dessert in refrigerator.

Makes 18 servings.

JAZZ IT UP:

Garnish with additional berries just before serving.

VARIATION:

Prepare as directed, using JELL-O Brand Strawberry Flavor Sugar Free Low Calorie Gelatin, COOL WHIP LITE Whipped Topping and reduced fat or fat free pound cake.

easy & elegant desserts

Creamy Lemon Nut Bars

Prep: 20 minutes plus cooling • Bake: 30 minutes

- ½ cup (1 stick) butter or margarine, softened
- ⅓ cup powdered sugar
- 2 teaspoons vanilla
- 1¾ cups flour, divided
- ⅓ cup **PLANTERS** Pecans, chopped
- 1 package (8 ounces) **PHILADELPHIA** Cream Cheese, softened
- 2 cups granulated sugar
- 3 eggs
- ½ cup lemon juice
- 1 tablespoon grated lemon peel
- 1 tablespoon powdered sugar

PREHEAT oven to 350°F. Line 13×9-inch baking pan with foil; spray with cooking spray. Mix butter, ⅓ cup powdered sugar and vanilla in large bowl. Gradually stir in 1½ cups of the flour and pecans. Press dough firmly onto bottom of prepared pan. Bake 15 minutes.

BEAT cream cheese and granulated sugar in medium bowl with electric mixer on high speed until well blended. Add remaining ¼ cup flour and eggs; beat until blended.

STIR in lemon juice and peel. Pour over baked crust in pan. Bake 30 minutes or until set. Remove from oven; cool completely. Sprinkle with 1 tablespoon powdered sugar; cut into 32 bars.

Makes 32 servings, 1 bar each.

HOW TO GRATE CITRUS PEEL:

Always wash and dry citrus fruit before grating. Move whole citrus fruit up and down on the side of the grater with the smallest holes to remove ONLY the surface of the fruit peel. (The inner white part is bitter.) Continue to grate fruit until you have the desired amount of grated peel, rotating fruit on the grater as necessary. Use this technique for grating any citrus fruit.

SUBSTITUTE:

Prepare as directed, using lime juice and grated lime peel.

easy & elegant desserts

114

3-STEP Mini Cheesecakes

Prep: 10 minutes plus refrigerating

2 packages (8 ounces each) **PHILADELPHIA** Cream Cheese, softened

½ cup sugar

½ teaspoon vanilla

2 eggs

12 **OREO** Chocolate Sandwich Cookies

1 kiwi, peeled, cut into 6 slices

36 blueberries (about ½ cup)

12 raspberries (about ⅓ cup)

PREHEAT oven to 350°F. Beat cream cheese, sugar and vanilla in large bowl with electric mixer on medium speed until well blended. Add eggs, 1 at a time, beating on low speed after each addition just until blended.

PLACE 1 cookie in bottom of each of 12 medium paper-lined muffin cups. Fill evenly with batter.

BAKE 20 minutes or until centers are almost set. Cool. Refrigerate 3 hours or overnight. Cut kiwi slices in half. Top each cheesecake with 1 kiwi half, 3 blueberries and 1 raspberry just before serving.

Makes 12 servings.

CHEESECAKE SQUARES:

Line 8-inch square baking pan with foil. Mix 1½ cups finely crushed OREO Chocolate Sandwich Cookies or HONEY MAID Honey Grahams with ¼ cup melted butter; press firmly onto bottom of pan. Prepare cheesecake batter as directed. Pour over crust. Bake and refrigerate as directed. Cut into 16 squares. Top evenly with the fruit mixture just before serving. Makes 16 servings, 1 square each.

Marble Brownies

Prep: 20 minutes • Bake: 40 minutes

- **1** package (20.5 ounces) brownie mix (do not use mixes that include a syrup pouch)
- **1** package (8 ounces) **PHILADELPHIA** Cream Cheese, softened
- **⅓** cup sugar
- **1** egg
- **½** teaspoon vanilla
- **½** cup **BAKER'S** Semi-Sweet Chocolate Chunks

PREHEAT oven to 350°F. Prepare brownie mix as directed on package; spread into greased 13×9-inch baking pan.

BEAT cream cheese with electric mixer on medium speed until smooth. Add sugar, mixing until well blended. Add egg and vanilla; mix just until blended.

POUR cream cheese mixture over brownie batter; cut through batter with knife several times for marble effect. Sprinkle with chocolate chunks.

BAKE 35 to 40 minutes or until cream cheese mixture is lightly browned. Cool; cut into squares.

Makes 32 servings, 1 square each.

SUBSTITUTE:

Prepare as directed, using PHILADELPHIA Neufchâtel Cheese, ⅓ Less Fat than Cream Cheese.

JAZZ IT UP:

After brownies have cooled, use a small, round cookie cutter, about 1 inch in diameter, to cut small, delicate petit four-type brownies.

American Berry No-Bake Cheesecake

Prep: 15 minutes plus refrigerating

- **2** packages (8 ounces each) **PHILADELPHIA** Cream Cheese, softened
- **⅓** cup sugar
- **2** cups thawed **COOL WHIP** Whipped Topping
- **1** **HONEY MAID** Graham Pie Crust (6 ounces)
- **1** pint (2 cups) strawberries, halved
- **⅓** cup blueberries

BEAT cream cheese and sugar in large bowl with electric mixer on medium speed until well blended. Gently stir in whipped topping.

SPOON into crust.

REFRIGERATE 3 hours or until set. Arrange strawberries and blueberries in rows on top of cheesecake to resemble flag. (Or arrange fruit in other desired design on top of cheesecake.) Store leftover cheesecake in refrigerator.

Makes 8 servings.

HEALTHY LIVING:

Looking for a reduced fat version of this summertime favorite? Save 10 grams of total fat, 6 grams of saturated fat and 90 calories per serving by preparing with PHILADELPHIA Neufchâtel Cheese, ⅓ Less Fat than Cream Cheese; COOL WHIP LITE Whipped Topping and a ready-to-use reduced fat graham cracker crumb crust (for a delicious 320 calories and 19 grams of fat per serving).

BEST OF SEASON:

Omit strawberries and blueberries. Prepare cheesecake as directed. Top with 2⅓ cups combined fresh raspberries and sliced peaches.

easy & elegant desserts

3-STEP Luscious Lemon Cheesecake

Prep: 10 minutes plus refrigerating • Bake: 40 minutes

2 packages (8 ounces each) **PHILADELPHIA** Cream Cheese, softened

½ cup sugar

½ teaspoon grated lemon peel

1 tablespoon fresh lemon juice

½ teaspoon vanilla

2 eggs

1 **HONEY MAID** Graham Pie Crust (6 ounces)

PREHEAT oven to 350°F. Beat cream cheese, sugar, peel, juice and vanilla with electric mixer on medium speed until well blended. Add eggs; mix just until blended.

POUR into crust.

BAKE 40 minutes or until center is almost set. Cool. Refrigerate at least 3 hours or overnight. Store leftover cheesecake in refrigerator.

Makes 8 servings.

VARIATION:

Prepare as directed, substituting lime juice for the lemon juice and grated lime peel for the lemon peel.

easy & elegant desserts

Chocolate Bliss Cheesecake

Prep: 30 minutes • Bake: 1 hour
Total: 5 hours 30 minutes (includes refrigeration)

18 **OREO** Chocolate Sandwich Cookies, finely crushed (about 1½ cups)

2 tablespoons butter or margarine, melted

3 packages (8 ounces each) **PHILADELPHIA** Cream Cheese, softened

¾ cup sugar

1 teaspoon vanilla

1 package (8 squares) **BAKER'S** Semi-Sweet Baking Chocolate, melted, slightly cooled

3 eggs

Cocoa powder and powdered sugar, optional

PREHEAT oven to 325°F if using a silver 9-inch springform pan, or to 300°F if using a dark, nonstick 9-inch springform pan. Mix cookie crumbs and butter; press firmly onto bottom of pan.

BEAT cream cheese, sugar and vanilla in large bowl with electric mixer on medium speed until well blended. Add melted chocolate; mix well. Add eggs, 1 at a time, mixing on low speed after each addition just until blended. Pour over crust.

BAKE 55 minutes to 1 hour or until center is almost set. Run knife or metal spatula around rim of pan to loosen cake; cool before removing rim of pan. Refrigerate 4 hours or overnight. Dust top of cheesecake with cocoa powder. Top with a heart-shaped stencil and sprinkle with powdered sugar, if desired. Store leftover cheesecake in refrigerator.

Makes 12 servings.

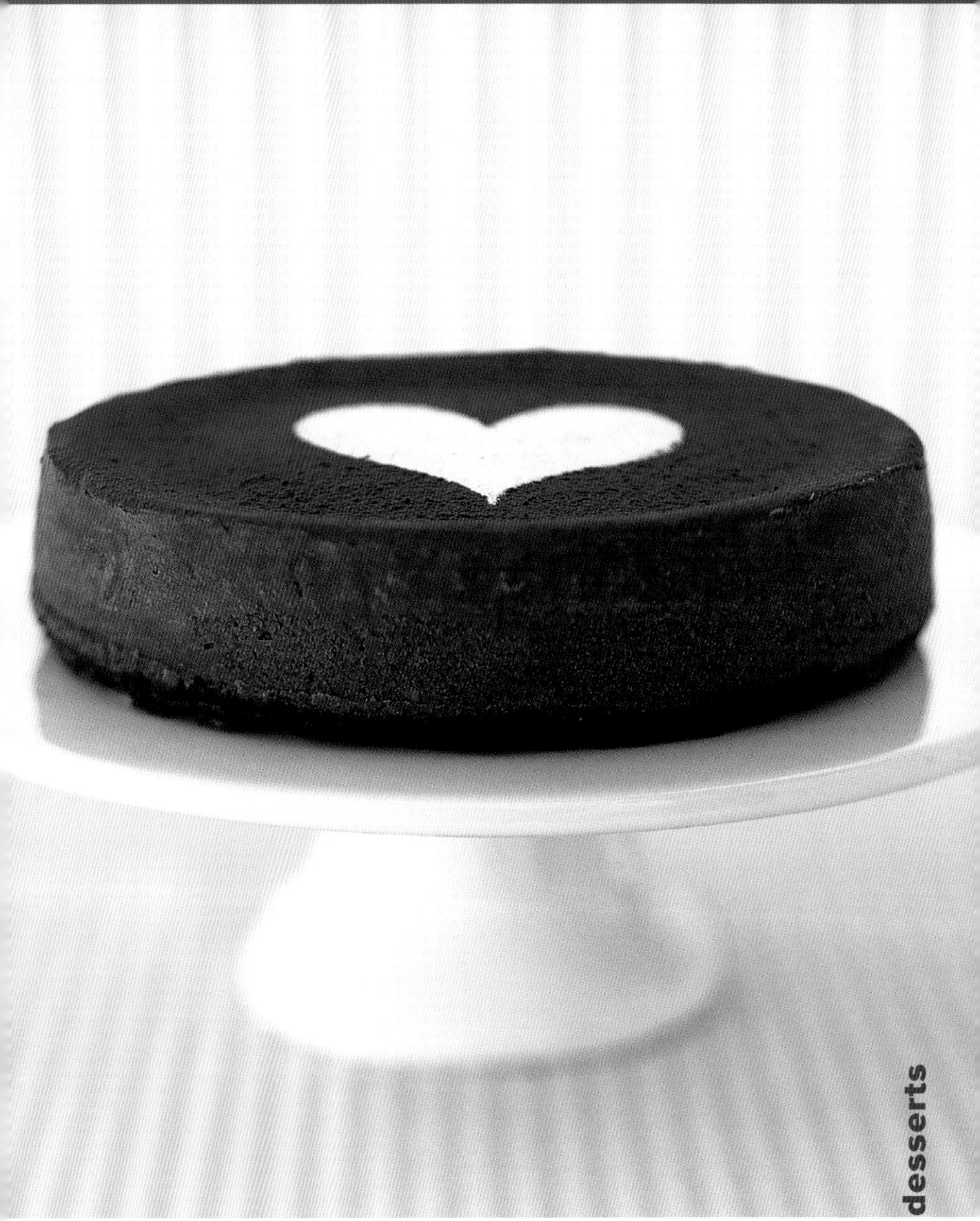

Banana Split Cake

Prep: 15 minutes plus refrigerating

1½ cups **HONEY MAID** Graham Cracker Crumbs

1 cup sugar, divided

⅓ cup butter, melted

2 packages (8 ounces each) **PHILADELPHIA** Cream Cheese, softened

1 can (20 ounces) crushed pineapple, drained

6 medium bananas, divided

2 cups cold milk

2 packages (4-serving size each) **JELL-O** Vanilla Flavor Instant Pudding & Pie Filling

2 cups thawed **COOL WHIP** Whipped Topping, divided

1 cup **PLANTERS** Chopped Pecans

MIX crumbs, ¼ cup of the sugar and the butter; press firmly onto bottom of 13×9-inch pan. Freeze 10 minutes.

BEAT cream cheese and remaining ¾ cup sugar with electric mixer on medium speed until well blended. Spread carefully over crust; top with pineapple. Slice 4 of the bananas; arrange over pineapple.

POUR milk into medium bowl. Add dry pudding mixes. Beat with wire whisk 2 minutes or until well blended. Gently stir in 1 cup of the whipped topping; spread over banana layer in pan. Top with remaining 1 cup whipped topping; sprinkle with pecans. Refrigerate 5 hours. Slice remaining 2 bananas just before serving; arrange over dessert. Store any leftover dessert in refrigerator.

Makes 24 servings, 1 piece each.

SUBSTITUTE:

Prepare as directed, using PHILADELPHIA Neufchâtel Cheese, ⅓ Less Fat than Cream Cheese; JELL-O Vanilla Flavor Fat Free Sugar Free Instant Reduced Calorie Pudding & Pie Filling; and COOL WHIP LITE Whipped Topping.

easy & elegant desserts

BEST-LOVED
CHEESECAKES

TIMELESS, CLASSIC CHEESECAKES
EVERYONE WILL LOVE

New York Cheesecake

Prep: 15 minutes plus refrigerating ● Bake: 40 minutes

1 cup crushed **HONEY MAID** Honey Grahams (about 6 grahams)

3 tablespoons sugar

3 tablespoons butter or margarine, melted

5 packages (8 ounces each) **PHILADELPHIA** Cream Cheese, softened

1 cup sugar

3 tablespoons flour

1 tablespoon vanilla

1 cup **BREAKSTONE'S** or **KNUDSEN** Sour Cream

4 eggs

1 can (21 ounces) cherry pie filling

PREHEAT oven to 325°F. Mix crumbs, 3 tablespoons sugar and butter; press firmly onto bottom of 13×9-inch baking pan. Bake 10 minutes.

BEAT cream cheese, 1 cup sugar, flour and vanilla with electric mixer on medium speed until well blended. Add sour cream; mix well. Add eggs, 1 at a time, mixing on low speed after each addition just until blended. Pour over crust.

BAKE 40 minutes or until center is almost set. Cool completely. Refrigerate at least 4 hours or overnight. Top with pie filling before serving. Store leftover cheesecake in refrigerator.

Makes 16 servings, 1 slice each.

JAZZ IT UP:

Omit pie filling. Arrange 2 cups mixed berries on top of chilled cheesecake. Brush with 2 tablespoons melted strawberry jelly.

Brownie Cheesecake

Prep: 15 minutes plus refrigerating • Bake: 40 minutes

1 package (19 to 21 ounces) brownie mix (13×9-inch pan size)

4 packages (8 ounces each) **PHILADELPHIA** Cream Cheese, softened

1 cup sugar

1 teaspoon vanilla

½ cup **BREAKSTONE'S** or **KNUDSEN** Sour Cream

3 eggs

2 squares **BAKER'S** Semi-Sweet Baking Chocolate

PREHEAT oven to 325°F. Spray 13×9-inch baking pan with cooking spray. Prepare brownie batter as directed on package; pour into prepared pan. Bake 25 minutes or until top of brownie is shiny and center is almost set.

MEANWHILE, beat cream cheese, sugar and vanilla in large bowl with electric mixer on medium speed until well blended. Add sour cream; mix well. Add eggs, 1 at a time, mixing on low speed after each addition just until blended. Gently pour over brownie layer in pan. (Filling will come almost to top of pan.)

BAKE 40 minutes or until center is almost set. Run knife or metal spatula around rim of pan to loosen side of dessert from pan; cool. Refrigerate at least 4 hours or overnight.

MELT chocolate as directed on package; drizzle over cheesecake. Refrigerate 15 minutes or until chocolate is firm. Cut cheesecake into 16 pieces to serve. Store any leftover cheesecake in refrigerator.

Makes 16 servings, 1 piece each.

best-loved cheesecakes

New York-Style Strawberry Swirl Cheesecake

Prep: 15 minutes plus refrigerating • Bake: 40 minutes

1 cup **HONEY MAID** Graham Cracker Crumbs

3 tablespoons sugar

3 tablespoons butter, melted

5 packages (8 ounces each) **PHILADELPHIA** Cream Cheese, softened

1 cup sugar

3 tablespoons flour

1 tablespoon vanilla

1 cup **BREAKSTONE'S** or **KNUDSEN** Sour Cream

4 eggs

⅓ cup **SMUCKER'S**® Seedless Strawberry Jam

PREHEAT oven to 325°F. Line 13×9-inch baking pan with foil, with ends of foil extending over sides of pan. Mix cracker crumbs, 3 tablespoons sugar and butter; press firmly onto bottom of prepared pan. Bake 10 minutes.

BEAT cream cheese, 1 cup sugar, flour and vanilla in large bowl with electric mixer on medium speed until well blended. Add sour cream; mix well. Add eggs, 1 at a time, mixing on low speed after each addition just until blended. Pour over crust. Gently drop small spoonfuls of jam over batter; cut through batter several times with knife for marble effect.

BAKE 40 minutes or until center is almost set. Cool completely. Refrigerate at least 4 hours or overnight. Lift cheesecake from pan using foil handles. Cut into 16 pieces to serve. Store leftover cheesecake in refrigerator.

Makes 16 servings, 1 piece each.

SUBSTITUTE:

Substitute 1 bag (16 ounces) frozen fruit, thawed, drained and puréed, for the ⅓ cup jam.

HEALTHY LIVING:

Save 80 calories, 10 grams of fat and 6 grams of saturated fat per serving by preparing with PHILADELPHIA Neufchâtel Cheese, ⅓ Less Fat than Cream Cheese and BREAKSTONE'S Reduced Fat or KNUDSEN Light Sour Cream (for a delicious 340 calories and 21 grams of fat per serving).

SMUCKER'S is a registered trademark owned and licensed by J.M. Smucker Company.

best-loved cheesecakes

132

White Chocolate Cheesecake

Prep: 35 minutes • Bake: 1 hour 30 minutes
Total: 6 hours 5 minutes (includes refrigeration)

¾ **cup sugar, divided**

½ **cup (1 stick) butter or margarine, softened**

1½ **teaspoons vanilla, divided**

1 **cup flour**

4 **packages (8 ounces each) PHILADELPHIA Cream Cheese, softened**

2 **packages (6 squares each) BAKER'S Premium White Baking Chocolate, melted and slightly cooled**

4 **eggs**

Raspberries and mint leaves, optional

PREHEAT oven to 325°F if using a silver 9-inch springform pan, or to 300°F if using a dark nonstick 9-inch springform pan. Beat ¼ cup of the sugar, butter and ½ teaspoon of the vanilla in small bowl with electric mixer on medium speed until light and fluffy. Gradually add flour, mixing on low speed until well blended. Press firmly onto bottom of pan; prick with fork. Bake 25 minutes or until edge is lightly browned.

BEAT cream cheese, remaining ½ cup sugar and remaining 1 teaspoon vanilla in large bowl with electric mixer on medium speed until well blended. Add melted chocolate; mix well. Add eggs, 1 at a time, mixing on low speed after each addition just until blended. Pour over crust.

BAKE 55 minutes to 1 hour or until center is almost set. Run knife or metal spatula around rim of pan to loosen cake; cool before removing rim of pan. Refrigerate 4 hours or overnight. Top with raspberries and mint leaf before serving, if desired. Store leftover cheesecake in refrigerator.

Makes 16 servings.

Caramel-Pecan Cheesecake Bars

Prep: 15 minutes plus refrigerating • Bake: 40 minutes

1½ cups **NABISCO** Graham Cracker Crumbs

1 cup coarsely chopped **PLANTERS** Pecans, divided

2 tablespoons granulated sugar

¼ cup (½ stick) butter, melted

4 packages (8 ounces each) **PHILADELPHIA** Cream Cheese, softened

1 cup firmly packed brown sugar

2 tablespoons flour

½ cup **BREAKSTONE'S** or **KNUDSEN** Sour Cream

1 tablespoon vanilla

3 eggs

1 bag (14 ounces) **KRAFT** Caramels, divided

PREHEAT oven to 350°F. Line 13×9-inch baking pan with foil, with ends of foil extending over sides of pan. Mix graham crumbs, ½ cup pecans, granulated sugar and butter; press firmly onto bottom of prepared pan. Bake 10 minutes.

BEAT cream cheese, brown sugar and flour in large bowl with electric mixer on medium speed until well blended. Add sour cream and vanilla; mix well. Add eggs, 1 at a time, mixing on low speed after each addition just until blended. Place 36 of the caramels and 1 tablespoon water in microwaveable bowl. Microwave on HIGH (100%) 1 minute or until caramels are completely melted when stirred. Add to cream cheese batter; stir until well blended. Pour over crust.

BAKE 40 minutes or until center is almost set. Sprinkle cheesecake with remaining ½ cup pecans. Refrigerate at least 4 hours or overnight.

PLACE remaining caramels and additional 1 tablespoon water in microwaveable bowl. Microwave on HIGH (100%) 1 minute or until caramels are completely melted when stirred. Drizzle over cheesecake; let stand until set. Remove dessert from pan using foil handles; cut into 32 bars to serve. Store leftover bars in refrigerator.

Makes 32 servings, 1 bar each.

best-loved cheesecakes

Chocolate Vanilla Swirl Cheesecake

Prep: 15 minutes plus refrigerating • Bake: 40 minutes

20 **OREO** Chocolate Sandwich Cookies, crushed (about 2 cups)

 3 tablespoons butter, melted

 4 packages (8 ounces each) **PHILADELPHIA** Cream Cheese, softened

 1 cup sugar

 1 teaspoon vanilla

 1 cup **BREAKSTONE'S** or **KNUDSEN** Sour Cream

 4 eggs

 6 squares **BAKER'S** Semi-Sweet Baking Chocolate, melted, cooled

PREHEAT oven to 325°F. Line 13×9-inch baking pan with foil, with ends of foil extending over sides of pan. Mix cookie crumbs and butter; press firmly onto bottom of prepared pan. Bake 10 minutes

BEAT cream cheese, sugar and vanilla in large bowl with electric mixer on medium speed until well blended. Add sour cream; mix well. Add eggs, 1 at a time, beating on low speed after each addition just until blended. Remove 1 cup of the batter; set aside. Stir melted chocolate into remaining batter. Pour chocolate batter over crust; top with spoonfuls of remaining plain batter. Cut through batters with knife several times for swirled effect.

BAKE 40 minutes or until center is almost set. Cool. Refrigerate at least 4 hours or overnight. Use foil handles to lift cheesecake from pan before cutting to serve. Store any leftover cheesecake in refrigerator.

Makes 16 servings, 1 piece each.

JAZZ IT UP:

Garnish with chocolate curls just before serving. Use a vegetable peeler to shave the side of an additional square of BAKER'S Semi-Sweet Baking Chocolate and a square of BAKER'S Premium White Baking Chocolate until desired amount of curls are obtained. Wrap remaining chocolate and store at room temperature for another use.

Black Forest Cheesecake

Prep: 15 minutes plus refrigerating ● Bake: 40 minutes

20 **OREO** Chocolate Sandwich Cookies, crushed (about 2 cups)

3 tablespoons butter, melted

4 packages (8 ounces each) **PHILADELPHIA** Cream Cheese, softened

1 cup sugar

1 teaspoon vanilla

1 cup **BREAKSTONE'S** or **KNUDSEN** Sour Cream

6 squares **BAKER'S** Semi-Sweet Baking Chocolate, melted

4 eggs

2 cups thawed **COOL WHIP** Whipped Topping

1 can (21 ounces) cherry pie filling

PREHEAT oven to 325°F. Line 13×9-inch baking pan with foil, with ends of foil extending over sides of pan. Mix cookie crumbs and butter; press firmly onto bottom of prepared pan. Bake 10 minutes.

BEAT cream cheese, sugar and vanilla in large bowl with electric mixer on medium speed until well blended. Add sour cream and chocolate; mix well. Add eggs, 1 at a time, mixing on low speed after each addition just until blended. Pour over crust.

BAKE 40 minutes or until center is almost set. Cool. Refrigerate at least 4 hours or overnight. Lift cheesecake from pan, using foil handles. Top with whipped topping and pie filling. Store any leftover cheesecake in refrigerator.

Makes 16 servings, 1 piece each.

SIZE-WISE:

Sweets can add enjoyment to a balanced diet, but remember to keep tabs on portions.

OREO Cheesecake

Prep: 20 minutes plus refrigerating • Bake: 45 minutes

1 package (1 pound 2 ounces) **OREO** Chocolate Sandwich Cookies, divided

¼ cup (½ stick) butter or margarine, melted

4 packages (8 ounces each) **PHILADELPHIA** Cream Cheese, softened

1 cup sugar

1 teaspoon vanilla

1 cup **BREAKSTONE'S** or **KNUDSEN** Sour Cream

4 eggs

PREHEAT oven to 325°F. Line 13×9-inch baking pan with foil, with ends of foil extending over sides of pan. Place 30 cookies in food processor; cover. Process 30 to 45 seconds or until finely ground. Add butter; mix well. Press firmly onto bottom of prepared pan.

BEAT cream cheese, sugar and vanilla in large bowl with electric mixer on medium speed until well blended. Add sour cream; mix well. Add eggs, 1 at a time, beating just until blended after each addition. Chop remaining cookies. Gently stir 1½ cups of the chopped cookies into cream cheese batter. Pour over crust; sprinkle with the remaining chopped cookies.

BAKE 45 minutes or until center is almost set. Cool. Refrigerate 4 hours or overnight. Lift cheesecake from pan, using foil handles. Cut into 16 pieces to serve. Store leftover cheesecake in refrigerator.

Makes 16 servings, 1 piece each.

HOW TO BAKE IN SPRINGFORM PAN:

Preheat oven to 325°F if using a silver 9-inch springform pan (or to 300°F if using a dark nonstick 9-inch springform pan). Prepare crust as directed; press firmly onto bottom of pan. Prepare filling as directed; pour over crust. Sprinkle with chopped cookies as directed. Bake 1 hour or until center is almost set. Run small knife or small spatula around rim of pan to loosen cake; cool before removing rim of pan. Refrigerate 4 hours or overnight.

best-loved cheesecakes

Chocolate Truffle Cheesecake

Prep: 20 minutes plus refrigerating • Bake: 1 hour 10 minutes

18 **OREO** Chocolate Sandwich Cookies, finely crushed (about 1½ cups crumbs)

2 tablespoons butter or margarine, melted

3 packages (8 ounces each) **PHILADELPHIA** Cream Cheese, softened

1 can (14 ounces) sweetened condensed milk

2 teaspoons vanilla

1 package (12 ounces) **BAKER'S** Semi-Sweet Chocolate Chunks, melted, slightly cooled

4 eggs

PREHEAT oven to 300°F if using silver 9-inch springform pan (or to 275°F if using dark nonstick 9-inch springform pan). Mix cookie crumbs and butter; press firmly onto bottom of pan. Set aside.

BEAT cream cheese, sweetened condensed milk and vanilla in large bowl with electric mixer on medium speed until well blended. Add chocolate; mix well. Add eggs, 1 at a time, mixing on low speed after each addition just until blended. Pour over crust.

BAKE 1 hour 5 minutes to 1 hour 10 minutes or until center is almost set. Run knife or metal spatula around rim of pan to loosen cake; cool before removing rim of pan. Refrigerate at least 4 hours or overnight. Store leftover cheesecake in refrigerator.

Makes 16 servings, 1 slice each.

JAZZ IT UP:

Garnish with fresh raspberries just before serving.

MAKE IT EASY:

Use bottom of straight-sided glass to evenly press cookie crumb mixture onto bottom of springform pan.

JAZZ IT UP:

Add ¼ cup coffee-flavored liqueur along with the chocolate.

best-loved cheesecakes

New York Cappuccino Cheesecake

Prep: 25 minutes plus refrigerating • Bake: 1 hour 10 minutes

1 cup chocolate wafer cookie crumbs

3 tablespoons sugar

2 tablespoons butter or margarine, melted

5 packages (8 ounces each) **PHILADELPHIA** Cream Cheese, softened

1 cup sugar

3 tablespoons flour

1 tablespoon vanilla

3 eggs

1 cup **BREAKSTONE'S** or **KNUDSEN** Sour Cream

1 tablespoon **MAXWELL HOUSE** Instant Coffee

3 tablespoons coffee-flavored liqueur

PREHEAT oven to 350°F if using a silver 9-inch springform pan (or to 325°F if using a dark nonstick 9-inch springform pan). Mix crumbs, 3 tablespoons sugar and butter; press firmly onto bottom of pan. Bake 10 minutes.

BEAT cream cheese, 1 cup sugar, flour and vanilla in large bowl with electric mixer on medium speed until well blended. Add eggs, 1 at a time, mixing on low speed after each addition just until blended. Add sour cream; mix well. Stir instant coffee granules into liqueur until dissolved. Blend into batter. Pour over crust.

BAKE 1 hour and 5 minutes to 1 hour and 10 minutes or until center is almost set. Run knife or metal spatula around rim of pan to loosen cake; cool before removing rim of pan. Refrigerate 4 hours or overnight. Store leftover cheesecake in refrigerator.

Makes 16 servings.

Pumpkin Swirl Cheesecake

Prep: 20 minutes plus refrigerating • Bake: 55 minutes

25 **NABISCO** Ginger Snaps, finely crushed (about 1½ cups)

½ cup finely chopped **PLANTERS** Pecans

¼ cup (½ stick) butter, melted

4 packages (8 ounces each) **PHILADELPHIA** Cream Cheese, softened

1 cup sugar, divided

1 teaspoon vanilla

4 eggs

1 cup canned pumpkin

1 teaspoon ground cinnamon

¼ teaspoon ground nutmeg

Dash ground cloves

PREHEAT oven to 325°F if using a silver 9-inch springform pan (or to 300°F if using a dark nonstick 9-inch springform pan). Mix ginger snap crumbs, pecans and butter; press firmly onto bottom and 1 inch up side of 9-inch springform pan.

BEAT cream cheese, ¾ cup of the sugar and vanilla with electric mixer until well blended. Add eggs, 1 at a time, mixing on low speed after each addition just until blended. Remove 1½ cups batter; place in small bowl. Stir remaining ¼ cup sugar, pumpkin and spices into remaining batter. Spoon half of the pumpkin batter into crust; top with spoonfuls of half of the reserved plain batter. Repeat layers. Cut through batters with knife several times for marble effect.

BAKE 55 minutes or until center is almost set. Cool completely. Refrigerate 4 hours or overnight. Cut into 16 slices. Store leftover cheesecake in refrigerator.

Makes 16 servings, 1 slice each.

HOW TO PREPARE CHEESECAKE IN 13×9-INCH PAN:

Line 13×9-inch baking pan with foil, with ends of foil extending over sides of pan. Prepare cheesecake as directed. Bake at 325°F for 45 minutes.

HOW TO TEST CHEESECAKE DONENESS:

Check cheesecake doneness by gently shaking the pan. If the cheesecake is done, it will be set except for a small area in the center that will be soft and jiggly. Do not insert a knife into the center as this may cause the cheesecake to crack during cooling.

Chocolate Royale
Cheesecake Squares

Prep: 20 minutes plus refrigerating ● Bake: 50 minutes

24 **OREO** Chocolate Sandwich Cookies, crushed (about 2 cups)

¼ cup (½ stick) butter or margarine, melted

4 packages (8 ounces each) **PHILADELPHIA** Cream Cheese, softened

1 cup sugar

2 tablespoons flour

1 teaspoon vanilla

1 package (8 squares) **BAKER'S** Semi-Sweet Baking Chocolate, melted, slightly cooled

4 eggs

PREHEAT oven to 325°F. Mix crumbs and butter; press firmly onto bottom of 13×9-inch baking pan. Bake 10 minutes.

BEAT cream cheese, sugar, flour and vanilla in large bowl with electric mixer on medium speed until well blended. Add melted chocolate; mix well. Add eggs, 1 at a time, mixing on low speed after each addition just until blended. Pour over crust.

BAKE 45 to 50 minutes or until center is almost set. Refrigerate at least 4 hours or overnight. Cut into 32 squares to serve. Store leftover dessert squares in refrigerator.

Makes 32 servings, 1 square each.

HOW TO PRESS CRUMB MIXTURE INTO PAN TO MAKE CRUST:

Use bottom of a dry measuring cup to evenly press cookie crumb mixture onto bottom of pan.

best-loved cheesecakes

JAZZ IT UP:

Garnish with sifted powdered sugar and mixed berries just before serving, if desired.

JAZZ IT UP:

Add ¼ cup hazelnut liqueur with the melted chocolate.

New York-Style
Sour Cream-Topped Cheesecake

Prep: 15 minutes plus refrigerating • Bake: 40 minutes

1½ cups **HONEY MAID** Graham Cracker Crumbs

¼ cup (½ stick) butter, melted

1¼ cups sugar, divided

4 packages (8 ounces each) **PHILADELPHIA** Cream Cheese, softened

2 teaspoons vanilla, divided

1 container (16 ounces) **BREAKSTONE'S** or **KNUDSEN** Sour Cream, divided

4 eggs

PREHEAT oven to 325°F. Line 13×9-inch baking pan with foil, with ends of foil extending over sides of pan. Mix crumbs, butter and 2 tablespoons of the sugar; press firmly onto bottom of prepared pan.

BEAT cream cheese, 1 cup of the remaining sugar and 1 teaspoon of the vanilla in large bowl with electric mixer on medium speed until well blended. Add 1 cup of the sour cream; mix well. Add eggs, one at a time, beating on low speed after each addition just until blended. Pour over crust.

BAKE 40 minutes or until center is almost set. Mix remaining sour cream, 2 tablespoons sugar and 1 teaspoon vanilla until well blended; carefully spread over cheesecake. Bake an additional 10 minutes. Cool. Cover; refrigerate 4 hours or overnight. Lift cheesecake from pan, using foil handles. Garnish as desired. Store leftover cheesecake in refrigerator.

Makes 16 servings, 1 piece each.

SUBSTITUTE:

Prepare as directed, substituting 1½ cups finely crushed OREO Chocolate Sandwich Cookies for the graham cracker crumbs.

HEALTHY LIVING:

Great news! You'll save 80 calories, 9 grams of fat and 7 grams of saturated fat per serving by preparing with margarine, PHILADELPHIA Neufchâtel Cheese, ⅓ Less Fat than Cream Cheese and BREAKSTONE'S Reduced Fat or KNUDSEN Light Sour Cream (for a delicious 340 calories and 21 grams of fat per serving).

best-loved cheesecakes

PARTY LINE

APPETIZERS, DIPS, AND SMALL
BITES PERFECT FOR ENTERTAINING

BLT Dip

Prep: 15 minutes

1   package (8 ounces) **PHILADELPHIA** Cream Cheese, softened

¾   cup shredded or chopped romaine lettuce

2   plum tomatoes, seeded, chopped

4   slices **OSCAR MAYER** Bacon, crisply cooked, drained and crumbled

SPREAD cream cheese onto bottom of 9-inch pie plate.

TOP with lettuce and tomatoes; sprinkle with bacon.

SERVE with **WHEAT THINS** Snack Crackers or assorted cut-up fresh vegetables.

Makes 2 cups or 16 servings, 2 tablespoons each.

VARIATION:

Prepare as directed, using PHILADELPHIA Neufchâtel Cheese, ⅓ Less Fat than Cream Cheese and LOUIS RICH Turkey Bacon.

Sweet Fruit Dip

Prep: 10 minutes plus refrigerating

- **4** ounces (½ of 8-ounce package) **PHILADELPHIA** Cream Cheese, softened
- **1** cup whole berry cranberry sauce
- **1** cup thawed **COOL WHIP** Whipped Topping

BEAT cream cheese and cranberry sauce with electric mixer on medium speed until well blended. Gently stir in whipped topping; cover.

REFRIGERATE at least 1 hour or until ready to serve.

SERVE with strawberries, red and green grapes, pineapple, kiwi or pears, cut into bite-size pieces for dipping.

Makes 16 servings, 2 tablespoons each.

FUN IDEA:

This dip is great spooned over individual servings of cut-up fresh fruit.

SUBSTITUTE:

Prepare as directed, using PHILADELPHIA Neufchâtel Cheese, ⅓ Less Fat than Cream Cheese and COOL WHIP LITE Whipped Topping.

party line

Cheesy Chili Dip

Prep: 5 minutes ● Microwave: 1 minute

1 package (8 ounces) **PHILADELPHIA** Cream Cheese, softened

1 can (15 ounces) chili

½ cup **KRAFT** Shredded Cheddar Cheese

2 tablespoons chopped cilantro

SPREAD cream cheese onto bottom of microwaveable pie plate; top with chili and Cheddar cheese.

MICROWAVE on HIGH (100%) 45 seconds to 1 minute or until Cheddar cheese is melted. Sprinkle with cilantro.

SERVE with **RITZ** Crackers.

Makes 3 cups or 24 servings, 2 tablespoons each.

SERVE AS A TOPPER:

Place unwrapped block of cream cheese on microwaveable plate; top with chili and Cheddar cheese. Microwave and garnish with cilantro before serving as directed.

VARIATION:

Use your favorite variety of canned chili, with or without beans, regular or spicy.

party line

Mexican Dip

Prep: 10 minutes

---

1 package (8 ounces) **PHILADELPHIA** Neufchâtel Cheese, ⅓ Less Fat than Cream Cheese, softened

½ cup **TACO BELL HOME ORIGINALS** Salsa

½ cup **KRAFT** 2% Milk Shredded Reduced Fat Cheddar Cheese

2 green onions, sliced (about ¼ cup)

WHEAT THINS Reduced Fat Baked Snack Crackers

SPREAD Neufchâtel cheese onto bottom of 9-inch pie plate.

TOP with layers of salsa, Cheddar cheese and onions.

SERVE with the crackers.

Makes 1⅔ cups dip or 13 servings,
2 tablespoons dip and 16 crackers each.

HOW TO SOFTEN NEUFCHÂTEL CHEESE:

Place unwrapped package of Neufchâtel cheese on microwaveable plate. Microwave on HIGH (100%) 20 to 30 seconds or until slightly softened.

TACO BELL Logo and HOME ORIGINALS are trademarks owned and licensed by Taco Bell Corp.

party line

Tomato-Basil Dip

Prep: 10 minutes

1 package (8 ounces) **PHILADELPHIA** Neufchâtel Cheese, ⅓ Less Fat than Cream Cheese, softened

2 plum tomatoes, seeded, chopped

2 tablespoons **KRAFT** Zesty Italian Dressing

2 tablespoons **KRAFT** Shredded Parmesan Cheese

1 tablespoons finely chopped fresh basil

SPREAD Neufchâtel cheese onto bottom of 9-inch pie plate.

MIX tomatoes and dressing; spoon over Neufchâtel cheese. Sprinkle with the Parmesan cheese and basil.

SERVE with **WHEAT THINS** Snack Crackers or assorted cut-up fresh vegetables.

Makes 1¾ cups or 14 servings, 2 tablespoons each.

VARIATION:

Prepare as directed, substituting KRAFT Balsamic Vinaigrette Dressing for Italian dressing.

Shrimp Cocktail Dip

Prep: 10 minutes

- **1** package (8 ounces) **PHILADELPHIA** Cream Cheese, softened
- **¾** pound cooked shrimp, chopped (about 2 cups)
- **¾** cup **KRAFT** Cocktail Sauce
- **¼** cup **KRAFT** Shredded Parmesan Cheese
- **¼** cup sliced green onions

SPREAD cream cheese onto bottom of 9-inch pie plate. Toss shrimp with cocktail sauce; spoon over cream cheese.

SPRINKLE with Parmesan cheese and onions.

SERVE with **WHEAT THINS** Snack Crackers.

Makes 3 cups or 24 servings, 2 tablespoons each.

SUBSTITUTE:

Substitute **1** package (8 ounces) imitation crabmeat, coarsely chopped, for shrimp.

Creamy Coconut Dip

Prep: 5 minutes plus refrigerating

- **1** package (8 ounces) **PHILADELPHIA** Cream Cheese, softened
- **1** can (15 ounces) cream of coconut
- **1** tub (16 ounces) **COOL WHIP** Whipped Topping, thawed

BEAT cream cheese and cream of coconut in large bowl with wire whisk until well blended.

ADD whipped topping; gently stir until well blended. Cover. Refrigerate several hours or until chilled.

SERVE with **HONEY MAID** Grahams Honey Sticks, **HONEY MAID** Honey Grahams or cut-up fresh fruit.

Makes 48 servings, 2 tablespoons each.

JAZZ IT UP:

Garnish with toasted **BAKER'S ANGEL FLAKE** Coconut just before serving.

party line

Garden Vegetable Dip

Prep: 10 minutes plus refrigerating

2 packages (8 ounces each) **PHILADELPHIA** Cream Cheese, softened

½ cup **KRAFT** Blue Cheese Dressing

½ cup finely chopped broccoli

1 medium carrot, shredded

MIX cream cheese and dressing until well blended. Stir in vegetables; cover.

REFRIGERATE several hours or until chilled.

SERVE with assorted **NABISCO** Crackers.

Makes 20 servings, 2 tablespoons each.

BEST OF SEASON:

Take advantage of the fresh seasonal vegetables that are available. Cut up zucchini, cucumbers and bell peppers to serve as dippers with this creamy dip.

VARIATION:

Prepare as directed, using PHILADELPHIA Neufchâtel Cheese, ⅓ Less Fat than Cream Cheese and KRAFT Light Blue Cheese Reduced Fat Dressing.

Bacon Appetizer Crescents

Prep: 30 minutes • Bake: 15 minutes

1 package (8 ounces) **PHILADELPHIA** Cream Cheese, softened

8 slices **OSCAR MAYER** Bacon, crisply cooked, crumbled

⅓ cup **KRAFT** 100% Grated Parmesan Cheese

¼ cup finely chopped onion

2 tablespoons chopped fresh parsley

1 tablespoon milk

2 cans (8 ounces each) refrigerated crescent dinner rolls

PREHEAT oven to 375°F. Mix cream cheese, bacon, Parmesan cheese, onions, parsley and milk until well blended; set aside.

SEPARATE each can of dough into 8 triangles. Spread each triangle with 1 rounded tablespoonful of cream cheese mixture. Cut each triangle lengthwise into 3 narrow triangles. Roll up, starting at wide ends. Place point-side down on greased baking sheet.

BAKE 12 to 15 minutes or until golden brown. Serve warm.

Makes 4 dozen or 24 servings, 2 crescents each.

JAZZ IT UP:

Sprinkle lightly with poppy seeds before baking.

Mini New Potato Bites

Prep: 30 minutes plus refrigerating

1½ pounds new potatoes (about 15 potatoes)

4 ounces (½ of 8-ounce package) **PHILADELPHIA** Cream Cheese, softened

2 tablespoons **BREAKSTONE'S** or **KNUDSEN** Sour Cream

2 tablespoons **KRAFT** 100% Grated Parmesan Cheese

4 slices **OSCAR MAYER** Bacon, cooked, crumbled

2 tablespoons snipped fresh chives

PLACE potatoes in large saucepan; add enough water to cover. Bring to boil. Reduce heat to medium-low; cook 15 minutes or until potatoes are tender.

MEANWHILE, mix cream cheese, sour cream and Parmesan cheese; cover. Refrigerate until ready to use.

DRAIN potatoes. Cool slightly. Cut potatoes in half; cut small piece from bottom of each potato half so potato lies flat. Place on serving platter. Top each potato half with 1 teaspoon of the cream cheese mixture. Sprinkle with bacon and chives.

Makes 15 servings, 2 topped potato halves each.

MAKE AHEAD:

These potatoes are delicious served hot or cold.

SUBSTITUTE:

Substitute PHILADELPHIA Chive & Onion Cream Cheese Spread for the regular cream cheese for added flavor.

Three Pepper Quesadillas

Prep: 20 minutes • Bake: 10 minutes

1 cup thin green bell pepper strips

1 cup thin red bell pepper strips

1 cup thin yellow bell pepper strips

½ cup thin onion slices

⅓ cup butter or margarine

½ teaspoon ground cumin

1 package (8 ounces) **PHILADELPHIA** Cream Cheese, softened

1 package (8 ounces) **KRAFT** Shredded Sharp Cheddar Cheese

10 **TACO BELL HOME ORIGINALS** Flour Tortillas

1 jar (16 ounces) **TACO BELL HOME ORIGINALS** Thick 'N Chunky Salsa

PREHEAT oven to 425°F. Cook and stir peppers and onion in butter in large skillet on medium-high heat until crisp-tender. Stir in cumin. Drain, reserving liquid.

BEAT cream cheese and Cheddar cheese with electric mixer on medium speed until well blended. Spoon 2 tablespoons cheese mixture onto each tortilla; top each evenly with pepper mixture. Fold tortillas in half; place on ungreased baking sheet. Brush with reserved liquid.

BAKE 10 minutes or until heated through. Cut each tortilla into thirds. Serve warm with salsa.

Makes 30 servings, 1 piece each.

MAKE AHEAD:

Prepare as directed except for baking; cover. Refrigerate. When ready to serve, bake, uncovered, at 425°F for 15 to 20 minutes or until heated through.

Blue Cheese Mushrooms

Prep: 30 minutes • Broil: 3 minutes

1 pound medium fresh mushrooms

¼ cup sliced green onions

1 tablespoon butter or margarine

1 package (4 ounces) **ATHENOS** Crumbled Blue Cheese

3 ounces **PHILADELPHIA** Cream Cheese, softened

PREHEAT broiler. Remove stems from mushrooms; chop stems. Cook and stir stems and onions in butter in small skillet on medium heat until tender.

ADD blue cheese and cream cheese; mix well. Spoon evenly into mushroom caps; place on rack of broiler pan.

BROIL 2 to 3 minutes or until golden brown. Serve warm.

Makes about 2 dozen or 24 servings, 1 mushroom each.

Baked Crab Rangoon

Prep: 20 minutes ● Bake: 20 minutes

1 can (6 ounces) white crabmeat, drained, flaked

4 ounces (½ of 8-ounce package) **PHILADELPHIA** Neufchâtel Cheese, ⅓ Less Fat than Cream Cheese, softened

¼ cup thinly sliced green onions

¼ cup **KRAFT** Mayo Light Mayonnaise

12 wonton wrappers

PREHEAT oven to 350°F. Mix crabmeat, Neufchâtel cheese, onions and mayo.

SPRAY 12 medium muffin cups with cooking spray. Gently place 1 wonton wrapper in each cup, allowing edges of wrappers to extend above sides of cups. Fill evenly with crabmeat mixture.

BAKE 18 to 20 minutes or until edges are golden brown and filling is heated through. Serve warm. Garnish with sliced green onions, if desired.

Makes 12 servings, 1 wonton each.

FOOD FACTS:

Wonton wrappers are usually found in the grocery store in the refrigerated section of the produce department.

FOR MINI CRAB RANGOONS:

Use **24** wonton wrappers. Gently place 1 wonton wrapper in each of 24 miniature muffin cups sprayed with cooking spray. Fill evenly with crabmeat mixture and bake as directed. Makes **12** servings, 2 appetizers each.

Party Cheese Ball

Prep: 15 minutes plus refrigerating

- 2 packages (8 ounces each) **PHILADELPHIA** Cream Cheese, softened
- 1 package (8 ounces) **KRAFT** Shredded Sharp Cheddar Cheese
- 1 tablespoon finely chopped onions
- 1 tablespoon chopped red bell peppers
- 2 teaspoons Worcestershire sauce
- 1 teaspoon lemon juice

  Dash ground red pepper (cayenne)

  Dash salt

- 1 cup chopped **PLANTERS** Pecans

BEAT cream cheese and Cheddar cheese in small bowl with electric mixer on medium speed until well blended.

MIX in all remaining ingredients except pecans; cover. Refrigerate several hours or overnight.

SHAPE into ball; roll in pecans. Serve with assorted **NABISCO** Crackers.

Makes 24 servings, 2 tablespoons each.

VARIATION:

Mix cream cheese mixture as directed; shape into log or 24 small balls, each about 1 inch in diameter. Roll in pecans until evenly coated. Serve as directed.

SUBSTITUTE:

Substitute pimientos for the red bell peppers.

Deviled Ham Finger Sandwiches

Prep: 15 minutes

- **1** package (8 ounces) **PHILADELPHIA** Cream Cheese, softened
- **1** can (4.25 ounces) deviled ham
- **¼** cup **KRAFT** Mayo Real Mayonnaise
- **10** small stuffed green olives, finely chopped
- **36** slices white bread, crusts removed

MIX cream cheese, ham, mayo and olives until well blended.

SPREAD each of 18 of the bread slices with about 2 tablespoons of the cream cheese mixture. Cover with remaining bread slices to make 18 sandwiches.

CUT each sandwich into quarters.

Makes 18 servings,
4 sandwich quarters each.

MAKE AHEAD:

Prepare cream cheese mixture as directed. Cover and refrigerate up to 5 days. Spread onto bread slices and continue as directed. For easier spreading, mix 1 tablespoon milk with chilled cream cheese mixture before spreading onto bread slices. Or prepare sandwiches as directed, but do not cut into quarters. Wrap in plastic wrap. Refrigerate until ready to serve. Cut into quarters just before serving.

SUBSTITUTE:

Substitute MIRACLE WHIP Dressing for the mayo.

Savory Bruschetta

Prep: 25 minutes

¼ cup olive oil

1 clove garlic, minced

1 loaf (1 pound) French bread, cut in half lengthwise

1 package (8 ounces) **PHILADELPHIA** Cream Cheese, softened

3 tablespoons **KRAFT** 100% Grated Parmesan Cheese

2 tablespoons chopped pitted ripe olives

1 cup chopped, seeded plum tomatoes

¼ cup chopped fresh basil

PREHEAT oven to 400°F. Mix oil and garlic; spread onto cut surfaces of bread. Bake 8 to 10 minutes or until lightly browned. Cool.

MIX cream cheese and Parmesan cheese with electric mixer on medium speed until blended. Stir in olives.

SPREAD toasted bread halves with cream cheese mixture; top with tomatoes. Cut into 24 slices to serve. Sprinkle with basil.

Makes 2 dozen or 24 servings, 1 slice each.

SHORTCUT:

Prepare as directed, using 1 can (14½ ounces) diced tomatoes, drained, for the chopped fresh tomatoes.

Double-Strawberry Margarita Squares

Total: 6 hours 15 minutes (includes freezing)

1¼ cups crushed pretzels

6 tablespoons butter or margarine, melted

1 package (8 ounces) **PHILADELPHIA** Cream Cheese, softened

1 can (14 ounces) sweetened condensed milk

1 cup pureed strawberries

½ cup lime juice

1 tub (8 ounces) **COOL WHIP** Strawberry Whipped Topping, thawed

Sliced strawberries, optional

MIX pretzel crumbs and butter in 13×9-inch pan; press firmly onto bottom of pan. Refrigerate until ready to use.

BEAT cream cheese and condensed milk in large bowl with wire whisk until well blended. Add strawberries and lime juice; mix well. Gently stir in whipped topping; pour evenly over crust.

FREEZE at least 6 hours or overnight. Let stand at room temperature 15 minutes to soften slightly. Cut into 16 squares. Garnish with sliced strawberries, if desired. Store leftover dessert in freezer.

Makes 16 servings, 1 square each.

SIZE-WISE:

Stick to the serving size. A small portion of these rich squares is all that is needed!

party line

Contents

191

209

235

263

Are you a chocolate lover?

Chocolate lovers can't live without the distinct flavor and rich, smooth texture of chocolate. They appreciate good quality chocolate and savor the experience of it slowly melting in their mouth. Chocolate lovers are always looking for new ways to prepare special desserts and treats using chocolate. If you're a chocolate lover, this magazine is for you. Whether it's semi-sweet, bittersweet, or white chocolate ideas you long for, BAKER'S is the brand you've trusted for quality chocolate for more than 225 years.

Whether you're celebrating a special occasion or looking for everyday treats, you'll find perfect chocolate recipes from the experts at BAKER'S right here at your fingertips. To help you find the best recipe to satisfy your chocolate craving, we've organized this magazine into the following sections:

■ **Chocolate Bliss** includes rich, decadent chocolate recipes to please any chocolate lover.

■ **Sweetheart Desserts** features recipes to share with that special someone on Valentine's Day, anniversaries, and other special occasions.

■ **Everyday Delights** are easy-to-make treats the whole family will love, including kid-friendly ideas.

■ **Entertaining Favorites** showcases party-perfect desserts that are sure to wow your guests.

■ **White Chocolate Wonders** includes cakes, candies, and other delicacies featuring creamy, dreamy white chocolate.

■ **Perfect Duos** pairs chocolate with classic flavors like peanut butter, strawberry, and hazelnut.

In addition, we've also included **a Tips & Techniques** section to help you skillfully master the art of chocolate desserts. So, get ready to dazzle your loved ones with these delicious desserts from BAKER'S Chocolate—the brand you trust for baking.

Chocolate Bliss

Rich, decadent recipes to please any chocolate lover

MOLTEN CHOCOLATE CAKES

Prep: 15 minutes • Total: 30 minutes

1	package (6 squares) **BAKER'S** Bittersweet Baking Chocolate
10	tablespoons butter
1½	cups powdered sugar
½	cup flour
3	whole eggs
3	egg yolks
	Powdered sugar and raspberries (optional)

PREHEAT oven to 425°F. Grease six (6-ounce) custard cups or soufflé dishes. Place on baking sheet.

MICROWAVE chocolate and butter in large microwaveable bowl on HIGH 2 minutes or until butter is melted. Stir until chocolate is completely melted. Add powdered sugar and flour; mix well. Add whole eggs and egg yolks; stir with wire whisk until well blended. Divide batter evenly among prepared custard cups.

BAKE 14 to 15 minutes or until cakes are firm around the edges but soft in the centers. Let stand 1 minute. Run small knife around cakes to loosen. Immediately invert cakes onto serving plate. Sprinkle lightly with additional powdered sugar and garnish with raspberries, if desired. Cut each cake in half to serve.

Makes 12 servings, 1 cake half each.

RICH CHOCOLATE MOUSSE

Prep: 15 minutes • Total: 1 hour 15 minutes (includes refrigerating)

- ⅓ cup whipping cream
- 4 squares **BAKER'S** Bittersweet Baking Chocolate
- 1 teaspoon vanilla
- 1 tub (8 ounces) **COOL WHIP** Whipped Topping, thawed, divided

MICROWAVE cream in large microwaveable bowl on HIGH 1½ minutes or until cream comes to boil. Add chocolate; stir until completely melted. Blend in vanilla. Cool 5 minutes or until mixture comes to room temperature, stirring occasionally.

ADD chocolate mixture to 2 cups of the whipped topping; stir gently with wire whisk until well blended. Spoon evenly into 6 dessert dishes.

REFRIGERATE 1 hour or until set. Top with remaining whipped topping just before serving. Store leftover desserts in refrigerator.

Makes 6 servings, about ½ cup each.

CHOCOLATE-ORANGE MOUSSE: Prepare as directed, stirring 1 teaspoon grated orange peel into the mousse mixture before spooning into dessert dishes. Garnish with orange wedges, if desired.

DOUBLE-CHOCOLATE TRUFFLE DESSERT

Prep: 20 minutes • Total: 4 hours 20 minutes
(includes refrigerating)

1½   packages (12 squares) **BAKER'S** Semi-Sweet Baking
      Chocolate

4   squares **BAKER'S** Unsweetened Baking Chocolate

½   cup (1 stick) butter or margarine

½   cup corn syrup

1   teaspoon vanilla

1   tub (8 ounces) **COOL WHIP** Whipped Topping, thawed,
      divided

1   package (10 ounces) frozen strawberries, thawed, puréed

12   small fresh strawberries

LINE 8×4-inch loaf pan with plastic wrap. Microwave chocolates,
butter and corn syrup in medium microwaveable bowl on HIGH
2½ minutes or until chocolates and butter are completely
melted, stirring after 1½ minutes. Cool completely. Stir in
vanilla; cover. Refrigerate 30 minutes or until thickened.

REMOVE ½ cup of the whipped topping; place in small bowl.
Cover and refrigerate for later use. Gradually add remaining
whipped topping to chocolate mixture, stirring constantly until
well blended. Spoon into prepared pan.

REFRIGERATE 3 hours or freeze 1 hour. Unmold onto serving
plate; remove plastic wrap. Let stand 15 minutes. Top with
reserved ½ cup whipped topping. Cut into 12 slices. Place 1 slice
on each of 12 dessert plates; top each with 2 tablespoons of
the puréed strawberries and 1 fresh strawberry. Store leftover
dessert in refrigerator or freezer.

Makes 12 servings, 1 slice each.

HOW TO MAKE INDIVIDUAL DESSERTS: Prepare as directed, spooning chocolate mixture evenly into 18 paper-lined medium muffin cups. Remove paper liners before serving. Makes 18 servings, 1 dessert cup each.

BAKER'S CLASSIC CHOCOLATE FUDGE

Prep: 10 minutes • Total: 2 hours 10 minutes
(includes refrigerating)

2   packages (8 squares each) **BAKER'S** Semi-Sweet Baking Chocolate

1   can (14 ounces) sweetened condensed milk

2   teaspoons vanilla

1   cup chopped **PLANTERS** Walnuts

LINE 8-inch square pan with foil, with ends of foil extending over sides of pan. Set aside. Microwave chocolate and milk in large microwaveable bowl on HIGH 2 to 3 minutes or until chocolate is almost melted, stirring after 2 minutes. Stir until chocolate is completely melted. Blend in vanilla. Stir in walnuts.

SPREAD into prepared pan.

REFRIGERATE 2 hours or until firm. Lift fudge from pan, using foil handles. Cut into 48 pieces.

Makes 4 dozen pieces or 24 servings, 2 pieces each.

SUBSTITUTE: Substitute toasted **BAKER'S ANGEL FLAKE** Coconut for the chopped walnuts.

CHOCOLATE TRUFFLE PIE

Prep: 10 minutes • Total: 45 minutes

10   squares (1¼ packages) **BAKER'S** Semi-Sweet Baking Chocolate

½   cup whipping cream

4   eggs

½   cup sugar

¼   cup flour

1   cup thawed **COOL WHIP** Whipped Topping

PREHEAT oven to 325°F. Place chocolate squares in large microwaveable bowl. Add whipping cream. Microwave on HIGH 2 minutes or until chocolate is almost melted. Stir until chocolate is completely melted; cool slightly.

ADD eggs, sugar and flour; beat with wire whisk until well blended. Pour into lightly greased 9-inch pie plate.

BAKE 35 minutes or until outer half of pie is puffed but center is still slightly soft; cool. Top each slice with a dollop of whipped topping just before serving.

Makes 10 servings, 1 slice each.

MAKE AHEAD: **Prepare, bake and cool pie as directed. Cover and freeze up to 1 week. Thaw in refrigerator before serving.**

OUR BEST CHOCOLATE CHEESECAKE

Prep: 30 minutes • Total: 5 hours 35 minutes (includes refrigerating)

1½   cups crushed **OREO** Chocolate Sandwich Cookies
     (about 18 cookies)

2   tablespoons butter or margarine, melted

3   packages (8 ounces each) **PHILADELPHIA** Cream Cheese,
     softened

1   cup sugar

1   teaspoon vanilla

1   package (8 squares) **BAKER'S** Semi-Sweet Baking Chocolate,
     melted, slightly cooled

3   eggs

     Powdered sugar and raspberries (optional)

PREHEAT oven to 325°F if using a silver 9-inch springform pan (or to 300°F if using a dark nonstick 9-inch springform pan). Mix crushed cookies and butter; press firmly onto bottom of pan. Bake 10 minutes.

BEAT cream cheese, sugar and vanilla with electric mixer on medium speed until well blended. Add chocolate; mix well. Add eggs, 1 at a time, mixing on low speed after each addition just until blended. Pour over crust.

BAKE 45 to 55 minutes or until center is almost set. Run knife or metal spatula around rim of pan to loosen cake; cool before removing rim of pan. Refrigerate 4 hours or overnight. Top with powdered sugar and raspberries, if desired.

Makes 16 servings.

HOW TO: This recipe can also be made in a greased, foil-lined 13×9-inch baking pan. Reduce the baking time by 5 to 10 minutes.

DECADENT FUDGY NUT BARS

Prep: 25 minutes • Total: 40 minutes

4 squares **BAKER'S** Unsweetened Baking Chocolate

¼ cup (½ stick) butter or margarine

¾ cup sugar

2 eggs

1 teaspoon vanilla

2 tablespoons flour

½ cup chopped **PLANTERS** Pecan Pieces

½ cup **HONEY MAID** Graham Cracker Crumbs

1 tablespoon sugar

2 tablespoons butter, melted

PREHEAT oven to 400°F. Microwave chocolate and ¼ cup butter in large microwaveable bowl on HIGH 1 minute or until butter is melted. Stir until chocolate is completely melted. Add ¾ cup sugar; mix well. Blend in eggs and vanilla. Stir in flour until well blended. Stir in pecans; set aside.

MIX graham crumbs, 1 tablespoon sugar and 2 tablespoons butter; press firmly onto bottom and ½ inch up sides of lightly greased 8-inch square baking pan. Spread chocolate mixture over crust.

BAKE 15 to 20 minutes or until center is set. Cool completely before cutting into bars to serve.

Makes 1 dozen or 12 servings, 1 bar each.

VARIATION: For "NUT-LESS" BARS, prepare as directed, omitting the pecans.

DECADENT RASPBERRY BROWNIES

Prep: 20 minutes plus refrigerating • Total: 2 hours 25 minutes

4	squares **BAKER'S** Unsweetened Baking Chocolate
¾	cup (1½ sticks) butter or margarine
2	cups sugar
3	eggs
1	teaspoon vanilla
1	cup flour
¼	cup seedless raspberry jam
6	squares **BAKER'S** Semi-Sweet Baking Chocolate, chopped
¾	cup whipping cream

PREHEAT oven to 350°F. Line 13×9-inch baking pan with foil, with ends of foil extending over sides of pan. Grease foil. Microwave unsweetened chocolate and butter in large microwaveable bowl on HIGH 2 minutes or until butter is melted. Stir until chocolate is completely melted. Stir sugar into chocolate mixture until well blended. Add eggs and vanilla; mix well. Stir in flour until well blended. Spread into prepared pan.

BAKE 30 to 35 minutes or until toothpick inserted in center comes out with fudgy crumbs. (Do not overbake.) Cool in pan.

SPREAD jam over brownies. Microwave semi-sweet chocolate and cream in microwaveable bowl on HIGH 2 minutes or until simmering. Stir until chocolate is completely melted and mixture is well blended. Spread evenly over jam layer. Refrigerate 1 hour or until chocolate layer is set. Lift dessert from pan, using foil handles. Cut into 32 brownies to serve.

Makes 32 servings, 1 brownie each.

JAZZ IT UP: Bake and glaze brownies as directed. Remove from pan; cut into diamond-shaped bars. Garnish each bar with a fresh raspberry.

BITTERSWEET CHOCOLATE TRUFFLES

Prep: 15 minutes plus refrigerating

2   tablespoons **MAXWELL HOUSE** Instant Coffee, any variety

¾   cup whipping cream

¼   cup (½ stick) butter or margarine, cut into chunks

3   tablespoons sugar

2   packages (6 squares each) **BAKER'S** Bittersweet Baking Chocolate, broken into chunks

½   teaspoon vanilla

¼   cup unsweetened cocoa powder

½   cup **BAKER'S ANGEL FLAKE** Coconut

ADD coffee granules to cream in large microwaveable bowl; stir until coffee is completely dissolved. Add butter and sugar; mix well.

MICROWAVE on HIGH 3 minutes or until mixture comes to full boil, stirring every 1½ minutes. Add chocolate and vanilla; stir until chocolate is completely melted.

REFRIGERATE 2 hours or until firm enough to handle. Shape into 24 balls, each about 1 inch in diameter. Roll in cocoa and/or coconut. Refrigerate until ready to serve. Store leftover truffles in refrigerator.

Makes 24 servings, 1 truffle each.

MAKE AHEAD: Truffles can be prepared up to 3 weeks ahead for gift giving. Store between layers of wax paper in airtight container in refrigerator.

Sweetheart Desserts

Festive recipes to share on Valentine's Day, anniversaries, and other special occasions

BLACK & WHITE HEART COOKIES

Prep: 20 minutes • Total: 2 hours (includes refrigerating)

½ cup (1 stick) butter, softened

⅔ cup sugar

1 egg

1½ teaspoons vanilla

1½ cups flour

1 teaspoon **CALUMET** Baking Powder

¼ teaspoon salt

1 package (8 squares) **BAKER'S** Semi-Sweet Baking Chocolate, melted

BEAT butter and sugar in large bowl with electric mixer on medium speed until light and fluffy. Blend in egg and vanilla. Mix flour, baking powder and salt. Add to butter mixture; beat until well blended. Cover and refrigerate 1 hour.

ROLL out dough to ⅛-inch thickness on lightly floured surface. Cut out with 2-inch heart-shaped cookie cutter. Place, 2 inches apart, on parchment paper-covered baking sheet. Refrigerate 30 minutes.

PREHEAT oven to 350°F. Bake cookies 10 minutes or until edges are lightly browned. Cool. Dip 1 side of each cookie in chocolate. Place on wire racks; let stand until chocolate is firm.

Makes about 4 dozen cookies or 24 servings, 2 cookies each.

JAZZ IT UP: Bake cookies and dip in chocolate as directed. Immediately sprinkle with red, white and/or pink-colored sprinkles. Place on wire racks; let stand until chocolate is firm.

HOMEMADE CHOCOLATE CUPS

Prep: 15 minutes • Total: 45 minutes
(includes refrigerating)

4 squares **BAKER'S** Semi-Sweet Baking Chocolate

MICROWAVE chocolate in microwaveable bowl on HIGH
2 minutes, stirring after 1 minute. Stir until chocolate is
completely melted.

PLACE 8 paper cupcake liners in medium muffin pan. Spray
each paper liner lightly with nonstick cooking spray. Fill evenly
with chocolate. Use back of spoon or pastry brush to spread
chocolate up sides of liners. Refrigerate at least 30 minutes or
until chocolate is firm.

PEEL paper liners off chocolate cups. Fill as desired just before
serving.

Makes 8 servings, 1 chocolate cup each.

CHOCOLATE MOUSSE-FILLED CUPS: Fill Chocolate Cups with
Rich Chocolate Mousse *(page 192)*, then garnish with Chocolate
Hearts *(page 281)*.

CINNAMON-CREAM FILLING: Gently stir ½ teaspoon ground
cinnamon into 1 cup thawed **COOL WHIP** Whipped Topping.
Sprinkle with additional cinnamon, if desired.

CHOCOLATE PEANUT BUTTER CUPS: Gently stir 1 cup thawed
COOL WHIP Whipped Topping into ¼ cup creamy peanut butter
until well blended. Garnish with chopped peanuts, if desired.

SWEETHEART CHOCOLATE PIZZA

Prep: 20 minutes • Total: 1 hour (includes cooling)

5	squares **BAKER'S** Semi-Sweet Baking Chocolate, divided
1	package (16.5 ounces) refrigerated sugar cookie dough
1	cup cold milk
1	package (4-serving size) **JELL-O** Chocolate Flavor Instant Pudding & Pie Filling
¼	cup powdered sugar
1	tub (8 ounces) **COOL WHIP** Whipped Topping, thawed, divided
1½	cups halved strawberries

PREHEAT oven to 375°F. Place 4 of the chocolate squares in medium microwaveable bowl. Microwave on HIGH 2 minutes, stirring after 1 minute. Stir until completely melted. Add cookie dough; mix until well blended. Press onto bottom of ungreased 12-inch pizza pan. Bake 10 minutes. Cool completely.

POUR milk into medium bowl. Add dry pudding mix and sugar. Beat with wire whisk 2 minutes or until well blended. Gently stir in half of the whipped topping. Spread evenly over crust.

SPREAD remaining whipped topping in heart shape over pudding layer. Decorate with strawberries. Melt remaining chocolate square as directed on package; drizzle evenly over dessert. Let stand until chocolate is firm. Cut dessert into wedges to serve. Store leftover dessert in refrigerator.

Makes 12 servings, 1 wedge each.

MAKE IT EASY: To make decorating the dessert easier, spoon whipped topping into resealable plastic bag; seal bag. Snip off small piece from one of the bottom corners of bag; pipe into heart shape on top of dessert.

WHITE CHOCOLATE-CHERRY BISCOTTI SWEETHEARTS

Prep: 30 minutes • Total: 54 minutes

- 2 cups flour
- 1½ teaspoons **CALUMET** Baking Powder
- ½ cup (1 stick) butter or margarine, softened
- ½ cup sugar
- 2 eggs
- 1 teaspoon vanilla
- 2 packages (6 ounces each) **BAKER'S** Premium White Baking Chocolate, chopped, divided
- ½ cup sweetened dried cherries
- ½ cup chopped **PLANTERS** Pecans (optional)

PREHEAT oven to 325°F. Lightly grease and flour large baking sheet. Mix flour and baking powder until well blended; set aside.

BEAT butter and sugar in large bowl with electric mixer on medium speed until light and fluffy. Add eggs and vanilla; mix well. Gradually add flour mixture, beating until well blended after each addition. Stir in 1½ cups of the chopped chocolate, cherries and pecans.

ROLL out dough to ¼-inch thickness on floured surface. Cut with 3-inch heart-shaped cookie cutter, rerolling dough scraps as needed. Place hearts, 2 inches apart, on prepared baking sheet.

BAKE 10 to 12 minutes or until lightly browned. Turn hearts over on baking sheet. Bake an additional 10 to 12 minutes or until slightly dry and golden brown. Remove to wire racks; cool completely.

MELT remaining chopped chocolate in microwaveable bowl on MEDIUM (50%) for 1 minute or until almost melted. Stir until chocolate is completely melted. Drizzle over hearts. Let stand until chocolate is firm.

Makes 26 servings, about 1 biscotti each.

PHILADELPHIA CHOCOLATE CHEESECAKES FOR TWO

Prep: 10 minutes • Total: 2 hours 10 minutes (includes refrigerating)

- 2 ounces (¼ of 8-ounce package) **PHILADELPHIA** Cream Cheese, softened
- 1 tablespoon sugar
- 1 square **BAKER'S** Semi-Sweet Baking Chocolate, melted
- ½ cup thawed **COOL WHIP** Whipped Topping
- 2 **OREO** Chocolate Sandwich Cookies

BEAT cream cheese, sugar and chocolate in medium bowl with wire whisk until well blended. Add whipped topping; mix well.

PLACE 1 cookie on bottom of each of 2 paper-lined medium muffin cups; fill evenly with cream cheese mixture.

REFRIGERATE 2 hours or overnight. (Or, if you are in a hurry, place in the freezer for 1 hour.)

Makes 2 servings.

JAZZ IT UP: Dust surface with cocoa powder. Top with heart-shaped stencil; dust with powdered sugar.

Everyday Delights

Easy-to-make treats the
whole family will love

SOFT & CHEWY CHOCOLATE DROPS

Prep: 20 minutes • Total: 1 hour 20 minutes (includes standing)

4 squares **BAKER'S** Unsweetened Baking Chocolate

¾ cup (1½ sticks) butter (margarine: see below)

2 cups sugar

3 eggs

1 teaspoon vanilla

2 cups flour

1 tub (8 ounces) **COOL WHIP** Whipped Topping (Do not thaw.)

6 squares **BAKER'S** Semi-Sweet Baking Chocolate

PREHEAT oven to 350°F. Microwave unsweetened chocolate and butter in large microwaveable bowl on HIGH 2 minutes or until butter is melted. Stir until chocolate is completely melted. Add sugar; mix well. Blend in eggs and vanilla. Add flour; mix well. Refrigerate 1 hour or until dough is easy to handle.

SHAPE dough into 1-inch balls; place, 2 inches apart, on greased baking sheets.

BAKE 8 minutes or just until set. (Do not overbake.) Let stand on baking sheet 1 minute; transfer to wire racks. Cool completely.

PLACE whipped topping and semi-sweet chocolate in microwaveable bowl. Microwave on HIGH 1½ minutes or until chocolate is completely melted and mixture is shiny and smooth, stirring after 1 minute. Let stand 15 minutes to thicken. Drizzle or spread over cookies. Let stand 40 minutes or until set.

Makes about 5 dozen or 30 servings, 2 cookies each.

TIP: For best results, use butter. If using margarine, add an additional ½ cup flour.

TEXAS SHEET CAKE

Prep: 25 minutes • Total: 45 minutes

CAKE

2 cups flour

2 cups granulated sugar

¼ teaspoon salt

1 cup plus 2 tablespoons water

¾ cup (1½ sticks) butter

2 squares **BAKER'S** Unsweetened Baking Chocolate

½ cup buttermilk

2 eggs

1 teaspoon baking soda

1 teaspoon vanilla

FROSTING

6 tablespoons butter

2 squares **BAKER'S** Unsweetened Baking Chocolate

6 tablespoons milk

1 package (1 pound) powdered sugar

1 teaspoon vanilla

CAKE:

PREHEAT oven to 400°F. Combine flour, sugar and salt in large bowl; set aside. Microwave water, butter and chocolate in microwaveable bowl on HIGH 2 minutes; stir. Continue microwaving 2 minutes or until chocolate is completely melted and mixture is well blended, stirring after each minute. Add to flour mixture; mix well. Add buttermilk, eggs, baking soda and vanilla; beat with electric mixer on medium speed 1 minute or until well blended. Pour into greased 15×10×1-inch baking pan.

BAKE 18 to 20 minutes or until wooden toothpick inserted in center comes out clean. Meanwhile, start to prepare the Frosting after 15 minutes.

FROSTING:

MICROWAVE butter, chocolate and milk in large microwaveable bowl on HIGH 2 minutes or until chocolate is completely melted and mixture is well blended, stirring after each minute. Add remaining ingredients; beat with electric mixer on medium speed until well blended.

SPREAD immediately onto warm cake. Cool completely before cutting into squares to serve.

Makes 24 servings, 1 square each.

SUBSTITUTE: Omit buttermilk. Place 1 tablespoon white vinegar in measuring cup. Add enough 2% milk to measure ½ cup. Let stand 5 minutes, then use as directed.

COCONUT-FUDGE BARS

Prep: 15 minutes • Total: 2 hours 30 minutes
(includes refrigerating)

1	cup (2 sticks) butter or margarine, divided
14	**HONEY MAID** Honey Grahams, finely crushed (about 2½ cups crumbs)
1	cup sugar
1	can (5 ounces) evaporated milk (about ⅔ cup)
1	package (10½ ounces) **JET-PUFFED** Miniature Marshmallows
1½	packages (12 squares) **BAKER'S** Semi-Sweet Baking Chocolate, coarsely chopped
1	cup chopped **PLANTERS** Walnuts
1	cup **BAKER'S ANGEL FLAKE** Coconut, toasted

LINE 13×9-inch pan with foil, with ends of foil extending over sides of pan. Grease foil. Melt ¾ cup (1½ sticks) of the butter; mix with graham crumbs. Press firmly onto bottom of prepared pan. Set aside.

PLACE remaining ¼ cup (½ stick) butter, the sugar, evaporated milk and marshmallows in large saucepan; bring to boil on medium heat, stirring constantly. Boil 5 minutes, stirring constantly. Add chocolate; cook until completely melted, stirring frequently. Pour immediately over crust; spread to evenly cover bottom of crust.

SPRINKLE with walnuts and coconut; press lightly into chocolate layer with back of spoon. Refrigerate 2 hours or until firm. Lift dessert from pan, using foil handles. Cut into 32 bars. Store in airtight container in refrigerator.

Makes 32 servings, 1 bar each.

CHOCOLATE-LAYERED NO-BAKE CHEESECAKE BARS

Prep: 15 minutes • Total: 3 hours 15 minutes
(includes refrigerating)

1½	cups **HONEY MAID** Graham Cracker Crumbs
¼	cup (½ stick) butter, melted
2	tablespoons sugar
1	package (8 squares) **BAKER'S** Semi-Sweet Baking Chocolate, divided
4	packages (8 ounces each) **PHILADELPHIA** Cream Cheese, softened
½	cup sugar
1	teaspoon vanilla
1	tub (8 ounces) **COOL WHIP** Whipped Topping, thawed

LINE 13×9-inch pan with foil, with ends of foil extending over sides of pan. Mix graham crumbs, butter and 2 tablespoons sugar. Press firmly onto bottom of prepared pan. Refrigerate while preparing filling.

MICROWAVE 6 of the chocolate squares in microwaveable bowl on HIGH 1 minute; stir until chocolate is completely melted. Cool slightly. Beat cream cheese, ½ cup sugar and the vanilla in large bowl with electric mixer on medium speed until well blended. Gently stir in whipped topping. Pour half of the batter into medium bowl; stir in melted chocolate. Pour over crust; cover with remaining plain batter.

MELT remaining 2 chocolate squares as directed on package; drizzle over batter. Refrigerate 3 hours or until firm. Using foil handles, remove cheesecake from pan; cut into bars. Store in tightly covered container in refrigerator.

Makes 16 servings, 1 bar each.

HOW TO NEATLY CUT DESSERT BARS: When cutting creamy-textured bars, such as cheesecake bars, carefully wipe off the knife blade between cuts with a clean damp towel. This prevents the creamy filling from building up on the blade, ensuring clean cuts that leave the edges intact.

FROZEN CHOCOLATE MOUSSE SQUARES

Prep: 15 minutes • Total: 6 hours 15 minutes (includes freezing)

12 **OREO** Chocolate Sandwich Cookies, crushed

¼ cup (½ stick) butter or margarine, melted

2 containers (8 ounces each) **PHILADELPHIA** Cream Cheese Spread

1 can (14 ounces) sweetened condensed milk

4 squares **BAKER'S** Semi-Sweet Baking Chocolate, melted

1 cup thawed **COOL WHIP** Whipped Topping

MIX crushed cookies and the butter in foil-lined 9-inch square pan. Press firmly onto bottom of pan to form crust.

BEAT cream cheese in large bowl with electric mixer on low speed until creamy. Gradually add milk, mixing well after each addition. Blend in chocolate. Gently stir in whipped topping. Spoon over crust; cover.

FREEZE at least 6 hours or overnight. Remove from freezer 15 minutes before serving to soften slightly. Cut into 16 squares to serve. Store leftover dessert in freezer.

Makes 16 servings, 1 square each.

HOW TO MAKE CHOCOLATE CURLS: See page 281.

CHOCOLATE-PECAN PIE BARS

Prep: 30 minutes • Total: 1 hour 5 minutes

- 2 cups flour
- 2 cups sugar, divided
- 1 cup (2 sticks) butter or margarine, softened
- ¼ teaspoon salt
- 1½ cups corn syrup
- 6 squares **BAKER'S** Semi-Sweet Baking Chocolate
- 4 eggs, lightly beaten
- 1½ teaspoons vanilla
- 2½ cups **PLANTERS** Chopped Pecans

PREHEAT oven to 350°F. Grease 15×10×1-inch baking pan; set aside. Beat flour, ½ cup of the sugar, the butter and salt in large bowl with electric mixer on medium speed until mixture resembles coarse crumbs. Press firmly onto bottom of prepared pan. Bake 20 minutes or until lightly browned.

MICROWAVE corn syrup and chocolate in large microwaveable bowl on HIGH 2½ minutes or until chocolate is almost melted, stirring after 1½ minutes. Stir until chocolate is completely melted. Add remaining 1½ cups sugar, the eggs and vanilla; mix well. Stir in pecans. Pour over hot crust; spread to evenly cover crust.

BAKE an additional 35 minutes or until filling is firm around the edges and slightly soft in center. Cool completely in pan. Cut into bars to serve. Store leftover bars in tightly covered container at room temperature.

Makes 4 dozen bars or 48 servings, 1 bar each.

USE YOUR STOVE: Prepare and bake crust as directed. Place corn syrup and chocolate in heavy 3-quart saucepan; cook on very low heat until chocolate is just melted, stirring constantly. Remove from heat. Continue as directed.

JAZZ IT UP: Melt 2 squares **BAKER'S** Semi-Sweet Baking Chocolate as directed on package; drizzle over cooled bars.

CHOCOLATE CRUNCH SQUARES

Prep: 5-minutes • Total: 24 minutes

1   tablespoon butter or margarine

3   cups (½ of 10½-ounce package) **JET-PUFFED** Miniature Marshmallows

½   cup peanut butter, divided

4   cups **POST HONEY BUNCHES OF OATS** Cereal

4   squares **BAKER'S** Semi-Sweet Baking Chocolate

GREASE 8-inch square pan lightly. Microwave butter and marshmallows in large microwaveable bowl on HIGH 30 seconds; stir. Microwave 30 seconds or until marshmallows are melted when stirred.

RESERVE 2 tablespoons peanut butter for frosting; set aside. Stir remaining peanut butter into marshmallow mixture. Immediately add cereal; toss until well coated. Press mixture into prepared pan.

MICROWAVE chocolate and reserved 2 tablespoons peanut butter in microwaveable bowl 1 to 1½ minutes, stirring after 30 seconds. Stir until chocolate is completely melted and mixture is smooth. Pour over cereal mixture; spread to cover. Refrigerate 15 minutes until frosting is set. Cut into 16 squares.

Makes 16 servings, 1 square each.

MAKE IT EASY: To pat cereal mixture into pan easily, lightly spray finger tips with cooking spray.

CHOCOLATE SUGAR COOKIES

Prep: 20 minutes • Total: 45 minutes

2 cups flour
1 teaspoon baking soda
¼ teaspoon salt
4 squares **BAKER'S** Unsweetened Baking Chocolate
1 cup (2 sticks) butter or margarine
1½ cups sugar, divided
1 egg
1 teaspoon vanilla

PREHEAT oven to 375°F. Combine flour, baking soda and salt; set aside.

MICROWAVE chocolate and butter in large microwaveable bowl on HIGH 2 minutes or until butter is melted. Stir until chocolate is completely melted. Add 1 cup of the sugar; mix well. Blend in egg and vanilla. Stir in flour mixture until well blended. Refrigerate 15 minutes or until dough is easy to handle. Shape into 1-inch balls; roll in remaining ½ cup sugar. Place, 2 inches apart, on ungreased baking sheets. (If flatter, crisper cookies are desired, flatten balls with bottom of clean glass.)

BAKE 8 to 10 minutes or until set. Cool on baking sheets 1 minute. Remove to wire racks; cool completely.

Makes about 3½ dozen or 21 servings, about 2 cookies each.

CHOCOLATE-CARAMEL SUGAR COOKIES: Omit ½ cup of the sugar. Prepare dough and shape into balls as directed. Roll in ½ cup finely chopped **PLANTERS** Pecans instead of the sugar. Place, 2 inches apart, on baking sheets. Make indentation in each ball. Bake as directed. Microwave 1 bag (14 ounces) **KRAFT** Caramels and 2 tablespoons milk in microwaveable bowl on HIGH 3 minutes or until caramels are completely melted, stirring after 2 minutes. Spoon evenly into centers of cookies. Drizzle with melted **BAKER'S** Semi-Sweet Baking Chocolate. Cool completely.

Entertaining Favorites

Party-perfect desserts sure to wow guests

SILKY CHOCOLATE CHEESECAKE

Prep: 15 minutes • Total: 5 hours 10 minutes (includes refrigerating)

1¾   cups **OREO** Chocolate Cookie Crumbs

2   tablespoons sugar

⅓   cup butter or margarine, melted

2   packages (4 ounces each) **BAKER'S GERMAN'S** Sweet
     Chocolate, divided

2   eggs

⅔   cup corn syrup

⅓   cup whipping cream

1½   teaspoons vanilla

2   packages (8 ounces each) **PHILADELPHIA** Cream Cheese,
     cubed, softened

PREHEAT oven to 325°F if using a silver 9-inch springform pan
(or to 300°F if using a dark nonstick 9-inch springform pan). Mix
cookie crumbs, sugar and butter until well blended. Press firmly
onto bottom and 1½ inches up side of pan. Microwave
1½ packages (6 squares) of the chocolate in microwaveable bowl
on HIGH 2 minutes, stirring after 1 minute. Stir until chocolate is
completely melted.

PLACE eggs, corn syrup, whipping cream and vanilla in blender
container; cover. Blend until smooth. With blender running,
gradually add cream cheese through small opening at top of
blender, blending until smooth. Add melted chocolate; cover.
Blend well. Pour into crust.

BAKE 50 to 55 minutes or until center is almost set. Run knife
or metal spatula around rim of pan to loosen cake; cool before
removing from pan. Refrigerate 4 hours or overnight.

MELT remaining 2 squares of chocolate as directed on package.
Drizzle over cheesecake just before serving. Store leftover
cheesecake in refrigerator.

Makes 12 servings.

FUDGY WALNUT PIE

Prep: 20 minutes • Total: 1 hour 45 minutes (includes refrigerating)

½   package (15 ounces) ready-to-bake pie crusts (1 crust)
1   package (8 squares) **BAKER'S** Semi-Sweet Baking Chocolate
¼   cup (½ stick) butter, softened
¾   cup firmly packed brown sugar
3   eggs
1   teaspoon vanilla
¼   cup flour
1   cup chopped **PLANTERS** Walnuts
½   cup **PLANTERS** Walnut Halves

POSITION oven rack in lower third of oven. Preheat oven to 375°F. Prepare pie crust as directed on package, using 9-inch pie plate; set aside. Microwave chocolate in large microwaveable bowl on HIGH 2 minutes. Stir until chocolate is completely melted; set aside.

BEAT butter and sugar in large bowl with electric mixer on medium speed until light and fluffy. Add eggs, 1 at a time, beating well after each addition. Blend in melted chocolate and vanilla. Add flour; mix well. Stir in chopped walnuts. Pour into crust. Arrange walnut halves over filling.

BAKE 25 minutes or until center of filling is set. Cool completely. Refrigerate at least 1 hour before serving.

Makes 12 servings.

CHOCOLATE GANACHE LAYERED TORTE

Prep: 40 minutes • Total: 1 hour 15 minutes

1   package (2-layer size) chocolate cake mix
1   package (8 squares) **BAKER'S** Semi-Sweet Baking
     Chocolate, melted
2/3 cup whipping cream
1/2 cup strawberry preserves
1 1/2 cups sliced strawberries
     Powdered sugar
     Sliced strawberry (optional)

PREHEAT oven to 350°F. Lightly grease 2 (9-inch) round cake pans. Prepare cake batter as directed on package; pour evenly into prepared pans. Bake 30 to 35 minutes or until wooden toothpick inserted in centers comes out clean. Cool in pans 10 minutes on wire racks. Loosen cakes from sides of pans with spatula or knife. Invert cakes onto racks; gently remove pans. Cool cakes completely.

MEANWHILE, place chocolate in small saucepan. Add cream; cook on low heat just until chocolate is melted, stirring frequently. Remove from heat; let stand 15 minutes or until completely cooled. (Ganache will thicken as it cools.)

CUT each cake horizontally in half with serrated knife to make 2 layers. Place 1 of the cake layers on serving plate; spread with about 3 tablespoons of the preserves. Top with 1/2 cup of the strawberries and 1/3 cup of the ganache, spreading ganache to completely cover cake layer. Repeat layers; top with the remaining cake layer. Sprinkle with powdered sugar just before serving. Garnish with sliced strawberry, if desired.

Makes 16 servings, 1 slice each.

VARIATION: Prepare as directed, using raspberry preserves and substituting fresh raspberries for the sliced strawberries.

TRIPLE-CHOCOLATE BLISS CAKE

Prep: 20 minutes • Total: 2 hours (includes cooling)

1	package (2-layer size) chocolate cake mix
1	cup **BREAKSTONE'S** or **KNUDSEN** Sour Cream
1	package (4-serving size) **JELL-O** Chocolate Flavor Instant Pudding & Pie Filling
4	eggs
½	cup oil
½	cup water
3	cups thawed **COOL WHIP** Whipped Topping
1	package (8 squares) **BAKER'S** Semi-Sweet Baking Chocolate
1½	cups raspberries

PREHEAT oven to 350°F. Lightly grease 12-cup fluted tube pan or 10-inch tube pan; set aside. Beat all ingredients except whipped topping, chocolate and raspberries in large bowl with electric mixer on low speed just until moistened. Beat on medium speed 2 minutes. Pour into prepared pan.

BAKE 50 minutes to 1 hour or until wooden toothpick inserted near center comes out clean. Cool in pan 10 minutes. Loosen cake from side of pan with knife or metal spatula. Invert cake onto serving plate. Gently remove pan. Cool cake completely. Transfer to serving plate.

MICROWAVE whipped topping and chocolate in microwaveable bowl on HIGH 1½ to 2 minutes or until chocolate is completely melted and mixture is well blended, stirring after each minute. Drizzle over cake. Let stand until firm. Spoon raspberries into center of cake. Store leftover cake in refrigerator.

Makes 18 servings, 1 slice each.

ORIGINAL BAKER'S GERMAN'S SWEET CHOCOLATE CAKE

Prep: 30 minutes • Total: 2 hours (includes cooling)

1   package (4 ounces)
    BAKER'S GERMAN'S Sweet
    Chocolate

½   cup water

2   cups flour

1   teaspoon baking soda

¼   teaspoon salt

1   cup (2 sticks) butter,
    softened

2   cups sugar

4   eggs, separated

1   teaspoon vanilla

1   cup buttermilk

    Coconut-Pecan Filling and
    Frosting *(recipe follows)*

PREHEAT oven to 350°F. Cover bottoms of 3 (9-inch) round cake pans with wax paper; grease sides of pans. Microwave chocolate and water in large microwaveable bowl on HIGH 1½ to 2 minutes or until chocolate is almost melted, stirring after 1 minute. Stir until chocolate is completely melted.

MIX flour, baking soda and salt; set aside. Beat butter and sugar in large bowl with electric mixer on medium speed until light and fluffy. Add egg yolks, 1 at a time, beating well after each addition. Blend in melted chocolate and the vanilla. Add flour mixture alternately with the buttermilk, beating until well blended after each addition.

BEAT egg whites in small bowl with electric mixer on high speed until stiff peaks form. Gently stir into batter. Pour evenly into prepared pans.

BAKE 30 minutes or until toothpick inserted in centers comes out clean. Immediately run small metal spatula around cake layers in pans. Cool in pans 15 minutes; remove layers from pans to wire racks. Remove and discard wax paper. Cool cake layers completely. Spread Coconut-Pecan Filling and Frosting between cake layers and onto top of cake.

Makes 16 servings.

Coconut-Pecan Filling and Frosting

Prep: 5 minutes • Total: 17 minutes

4	egg yolks
1	can (12 ounces) evaporated milk
1½	teaspoons vanilla
1½	cups sugar
¾	cup (1½ sticks) butter or margarine
1	package (7 ounces) **BAKER'S ANGEL FLAKE** Coconut (about 2⅔ cups)
1½	cups **PLANTERS** Chopped Pecans

BEAT egg yolks, milk and vanilla in large saucepan with wire whisk until well blended. Add sugar and butter; cook on medium heat 12 minutes or until thickened and golden brown, stirring constantly. Remove from heat.

ADD coconut and pecans; mix well. Cool to room temperature and of desired spreading consistency.

Makes about 4½ cups or 36 servings, about 2 tablespoons each.

WHITE CHOCOLATE-BERRY PIE

Prep: 20 minutes • Total: 1 hour 20 minutes (includes refrigerating)

½ package (15 ounces) ready-to-bake pie crusts (1 crust)

6 squares **BAKER'S** Premium White Baking Chocolate, divided

2 tablespoons milk

4 ounces (½ of 8-ounce package) **PHILADELPHIA** Cream Cheese, softened

⅓ cup powdered sugar

1 teaspoon grated orange peel

2 cups thawed **COOL WHIP** Whipped Topping

2 cups raspberries

PREPARE and bake pie crust in 9-inch pie plate as directed on package for unfilled 1-crust pie. Cool.

MICROWAVE 5 of the white chocolate squares and milk in large microwaveable bowl on HIGH 2 minutes or until chocolate is almost melted, stirring after 1 minute. Stir until chocolate is completely melted. Cool to room temperature.

BEAT cream cheese, powdered sugar and orange peel with electric mixer on low speed until well blended. Add to chocolate mixture; beat with wire whisk until well blended. Gently stir in whipped topping. Spread into pie crust; top with raspberries. Melt remaining chocolate square as directed on package; drizzle over raspberries. Refrigerate 1 hour or until ready to serve. Store leftover pie in refrigerator.

Makes 8 servings.

SUBSTITUTE: Substitute sliced strawberries for the raspberries.

CHOCOLATE FONDUE

Take ⅓ cup whipping cream and mix & match your recipe from these options...

Just follow our 3 simple steps:

BAKER'S Baking Chocolate options	flavoring choices
Bittersweet	2 tablespoons orange-flavored liqueur
Premium White	2 tablespoons peanut butter
Semi-Sweet	½ cup **JET-PUFFED** Miniature Marshmallows; ¼ cup chopped **PLANTERS** Dry Roasted Peanuts (stir in both after chocolate is melted)
Premium White	2 teaspoons grated lemon peel

1. **PLACE** 6 squares **BAKER'S Baking Chocolate**, whipping cream and **flavoring** in small microwaveable bowl.

2. **MICROWAVE** on HIGH 2 minutes or until chocolate is completely melted, stirring after each 1 minute. Spoon into shallow serving bowl.

3. **SERVE** warm with dippers such as strawberries, apple or pear slices, banana chunks, angel food or pound cake cubes, or assorted **NABISCO** Cookies.

Makes 8 servings, 2 tablespoons fondue each.

SUBSTITUTE: Substitute 2 teaspoons grated orange peel for the liqueur.

BAKER'S ONE BOWL BITTERSWEET TORTE

Prep: 20 minutes • Total: 1 hour

- 1 package (6 squares) **BAKER'S** Bittersweet Baking Chocolate, divided
- ¾ cup (1½ sticks) butter or margarine
- 1 cup sugar
- 3 eggs
- 1 teaspoon vanilla
- ⅓ cup flour
- ¼ teaspoon salt
- ½ cup chopped **PLANTERS** Pecans

PREHEAT oven to 350°F. Grease and flour 9-inch round cake pan. Line bottom of pan with wax paper; set aside.

MICROWAVE 4 of the chocolate squares and butter in large microwaveable bowl on HIGH 1½ to 2 minutes or until chocolate is almost melted, stirring after 1 minute. Stir until chocolate is completely melted. Add sugar; mix well. Blend in eggs and vanilla. Add flour and salt; mix well. Stir in pecans. Pour into prepared pan.

BAKE 40 minutes or until toothpick inserted in center comes out with fudgy crumbs. (Do not overbake.) Cool in pan 5 minutes. Run small knife around side of pan to loosen edge. Invert torte onto serving platter; remove wax paper. Melt remaining 2 chocolate squares. Drizzle over top of torte. Let stand until firm.

Makes 12 servings.

SUBSTITUTE: Substitute **BAKER'S** Semi-Sweet Baking Chocolate for the bittersweet chocolate.

White Chocolate Wonders

Sweet delicacies made with creamy, dreamy white chocolate

TWO-INGREDIENT WHITE CHOCOLATE MOUSSE

Prep: 10 minutes • Total: 2 hours 10 minutes (includes refrigerating)

1 package (6 squares) **BAKER'S** Premium White Baking Chocolate

1½ cups whipping cream, divided

White chocolate curls (optional)

MICROWAVE chocolate and ¼ cup of the cream in large microwaveable bowl on HIGH 2 minutes or until chocolate is almost melted, stirring after 1 minute. Stir until chocolate is completely melted. Cool 20 minutes or until at room temperature, stirring occasionally.

BEAT remaining 1¼ cups cream in chilled medium bowl with electric mixer on medium speed until soft peaks form. (Do not overbeat.) Add half of the whipped cream to chocolate mixture; stir with wire whisk until well blended. Gently stir in remaining whipped cream. Spoon evenly into 6 dessert dishes. Garnish with chocolate curls, if desired.

REFRIGERATE 2 hours or until ready to serve.

Makes 6 servings, about ½ cup each.

SPRING FRUIT TRIFLE

Prep: 15 minutes • Total: 45 minutes (includes refrigerating)

36 **NILLA** Wafers

2 tablespoons orange-flavored liqueur or orange juice

3 cups seasonal fresh fruit, such as sliced peeled kiwi, blueberries and/or sliced strawberries

3 cups cold milk

2 packages (4-serving size each) **JELL-O** Vanilla Flavor Instant Pudding & Pie Filling

1 package (6 squares) **BAKER'S** Premium White Baking Chocolate, melted, cooled slightly

1 tub (8 ounces) **COOL WHIP** Whipped Topping, thawed, divided

BREAK wafers coarsely into 2½-quart clear glass serving bowl. Sprinkle with liqueur; top with layers of fruit.

POUR milk into medium bowl. Add dry pudding mixes. Beat with wire whisk 2 minutes or until well blended. Refrigerate until pudding starts to thicken. Add chocolate; stir with wire whisk until well blended. Gently stir in half of the whipped topping. Spoon over fruit; top with the remaining whipped topping.

REFRIGERATE at least 30 minutes or up to 24 hours before serving. Store leftover dessert in refrigerator.

Makes 15 servings, ⅔ cup each.

HOW TO BLEND PUDDING WITH THE MELTED CHOCOLATE: Remove a small amount (about ½ cup) of the thickened pudding. Add to the melted chocolate; stir until well blended. Return to the remaining pudding; mix until well blended.

WHITE CHOCOLATE FUDGE

Prep: 20 minutes • Total: 2 hours 20 minutes
(includes refrigerating)

2 packages (6 squares each) **BAKER'S** Premium White
   Baking Chocolate
¾ cup sweetened condensed milk
1 cup coarsely chopped **PLANTERS** Almonds, toasted
½ cup dried cranberries
1 tablespoon grated orange peel

LINE 8-inch square pan with foil, with ends of foil extending over sides of pan; set aside. Microwave chocolate and milk in large microwaveable bowl on HIGH 2 to 3 minutes or until chocolate is almost melted; stir until chocolate is completely melted. Add almonds, cranberries and orange peel; stir until well blended.

SPREAD chocolate mixture into prepared pan. Refrigerate 2 hours or until firm.

LIFT fudge from pan, using foil handles. Cut into 48 pieces. Store in tightly covered container in refrigerator up to 3 weeks. (Do not freeze.)

Makes 4 dozen pieces or 24 servings, 2 pieces each.

WHAT TO DO WITH LEFTOVER SWEETENED CONDENSED MILK: Store leftover sweetened condensed milk in tightly covered container in refrigerator up to 1 week. Serve over cut-up fruit or hot cooked oatmeal. Or for extra flavor, stir into your cup of hot brewed coffee or tea instead of regular milk.

PASTEL MARBLE BARK

Prep: 20 minutes • Total: 1 hour 20 minutes
(includes refrigerating)

2 packages (6 squares each) **BAKER'S** Premium White
Baking Chocolate
Assorted food colorings

MICROWAVE each package of chocolate in separate medium
microwaveable bowls on HIGH 2 minutes, stirring after
1 minute. Stir until chocolates are completely melted.

MIX desired food coloring into each bowl of melted chocolate
until well blended. (Or, tint just 1 bowl of melted chocolate,
keeping second bowl of melted chocolate white.) Alternately
spoon tinted chocolates onto wax paper-covered baking sheet or
tray. Tap baking sheet on table top to evenly disperse chocolate.
Swirl colored chocolates with knife several times for marble
effect.

REFRIGERATE 1 hour or until firm. Break into pieces.

Makes about ¾-pound bark or 12 servings.

NOTE: Suggested amounts of food coloring to tint 1 package
(6 squares) BAKER'S Premium White Chocolate: Pink, 3 drops
red; pastel green, 3 drops green; pastel yellow, 3 drops yellow;
pastel blue, 5 drops blue.

WHITE CHOCOLATE FRUIT AND NUT CLUSTERS

Prep: 10 minutes • Total: 20 minutes

1   package (6 squares) **BAKER'S** Premium White Baking Chocolate

⅓   cup **PLANTERS** Sunflower Kernels

⅓   cup **PLANTERS** Slivered Almonds

⅓   cup dried cranberries

MICROWAVE chocolate in large microwaveable bowl on HIGH 2 minutes or until chocolate is almost melted; stir until chocolate is completely melted. Stir in remaining ingredients.

SPOON 1 teaspoon of the chocolate mixture into each of 48 miniature muffin cup liners. Refrigerate at least 10 minutes or until ready to serve.

Makes 12 servings, 4 clusters each.

SUBSTITUTE: Prepare as directed, substituting 6 squares **BAKER'S** Semi-Sweet Baking Chocolate for the white chocolate.

WHITE CHOCOLATE-RASPBERRY CAKE

Prep: 30 minutes • Total: 58 minutes

1   package (6 squares) **BAKER'S** Premium White Baking
     Chocolate, chopped
½   cup (1 stick) butter or margarine
1   package (2-layer size) white cake mix
1   cup milk
3   eggs
1   teaspoon vanilla
     White Chocolate-Cream Cheese Frosting
     (*recipe follows*)
2   tablespoons seedless raspberry jam
1   cup raspberries

PREHEAT oven to 350°F. Grease and flour 2 (9-inch) round cake pans; set aside. Microwave chocolate and butter in medium microwaveable bowl on HIGH 2 minutes or until butter is melted. Stir until chocolate is completely melted; cool slightly.

BEAT cake mix, milk, eggs, vanilla and chocolate mixture in large bowl with electric mixer on low speed just until moistened, scraping side of bowl frequently. Beat on medium speed 2 minutes or until well blended. Pour evenly into prepared pans.

BAKE 25 to 28 minutes or until toothpick inserted in centers comes out clean. Cool cakes in pans 10 minutes; remove from pans. Cool completely on wire racks. Place 1 cake layer on serving plate; spread with layers of ⅔ cup of the White Chocolate-Cream Cheese Frosting and the jam. Cover with remaining cake layer. Frost top and side of cake with remaining frosting. Top with raspberries just before serving. Store in refrigerator.

Makes 16 servings.

White Chocolate-Cream Cheese Frosting

Prep: 10 minutes • Total: 10 minutes

1   package (8 ounces) **PHILADELPHIA** Cream Cheese, softened

¼   cup (½ stick) butter or margarine, softened

1   package (6 squares) **BAKER'S** Premium White Baking Chocolate, melted, cooled slightly

1   teaspoon vanilla

2   cups powdered sugar

BEAT cream cheese and butter in large bowl with electric mixer on medium speed until well blended. Add melted chocolate and vanilla; mix well.

ADD sugar gradually, beating until light and fluffy after each addition.

Makes about 3 cups or 24 servings, 2 tablespoons each.

Perfect Duos

Desserts featuring classic chocolate pairings

MARBLE BARK

Prep: 15 minutes • Total: 1 hour 15 minutes (includes refrigerating)

- 6 squares **BAKER'S** Semi-Sweet Baking Chocolate
- 1 package (6 squares) **BAKER'S** Premium White Baking Chocolate
- 1 cup **PLANTERS** Chopped Pecans, toasted

MICROWAVE semi-sweet and white chocolates in separate microwaveable bowls on HIGH 2 minutes or until chocolates are almost melted, stirring after 1 minute. Stir until chocolates are completely melted.

STIR ½ cup of the pecans into each bowl. Alternately spoon melted chocolates onto wax paper-covered baking sheet or tray. Swirl chocolates together with knife for marble effect.

REFRIGERATE 1½ hours or until firm. Break into pieces. Store in tightly covered container at room temperature.

Makes 10 servings, 1 piece each.

CHOCOLATE-RASPBERRY TORTE

Prep: 20 minutes • Total: 1 hour 30 minutes
(includes refrigerating)

1½ packages (12 squares) **BAKER'S** Semi-Sweet Baking Chocolate, divided

¾ cup (1½ sticks) butter or margarine

1 package (4-serving size) **JELL-O** Raspberry Flavor Gelatin

½ cup sugar

3 eggs

⅓ cup flour

½ cup **PLANTERS** Chopped Pecans, toasted (optional)

1 tub (8 ounces) **COOL WHIP** or **COOL WHIP** French Vanilla Whipped Topping, thawed

Raspberries (optional)

PREHEAT oven to 350°F. Grease and flour 9-inch round cake pan; line bottom with wax paper. Microwave 4 squares of the chocolate and butter in large microwaveable bowl on HIGH 1½ to 2 minutes or until chocolate is almost melted, stirring after 1 minute. Stir until chocolate is completely melted. Stir dry gelatin mix and sugar into chocolate until well blended. Mix in eggs. Stir in flour and pecans until well blended. Pour into prepared pan.

BAKE 40 minutes or until toothpick inserted in center comes out with fudgy crumbs. (Do not overbake.) Cool in pan 5 minutes. Run small knife around side of pan to loosen edge. Invert onto serving platter; remove wax paper. Cool cake completely.

MELT 4 squares of the remaining chocolate in microwave on HIGH 1½ minutes or until almost melted, stirring after 1 minute. Stir until chocolate is completely melted. Spread on wax paper-covered baking sheet; refrigerate 30 minutes.

MEANWHILE, melt remaining 4 squares chocolate in microwaveable bowl on HIGH 1½ minutes or until almost melted, stirring after 1 minute. Stir until chocolate is completely melted; stir in whipped topping until smooth. Frost cake with whipped chocolate mixture.

REMOVE chocolate on baking sheet from refrigerator; using sharp knife, cut into 1½- to 2-inch irregular-shaped pieces. Remove chocolate pieces from wax paper; arrange on top of cake. Garnish with raspberries, if desired. Store cake in refrigerator.

Makes 14 servings.

> *VARIATION:* Not a raspberry lover? Omit raspberry gelatin. Prepare as directed, using 1 cup sugar.

PINWHEEL COOKIES

Prep: 20 minutes • Total: 1 hour 2 minutes
(includes refrigerating)

1   package (8 ounces) **PHILADELPHIA** Cream Cheese, softened
¾   cup (1½ sticks) butter, softened
1   cup sugar
2   teaspoons vanilla
2¼   cups flour
½   teaspoon baking soda
2   squares **BAKER'S** Semi-Sweet Baking Chocolate, melted

BEAT cream cheese, butter, sugar and vanilla in large bowl with electric mixer on medium speed until well blended. Add flour and baking soda; mix well. Cover. Refrigerate 30 minutes.

PREHEAT oven to 350°F. Divide dough in half. Add melted chocolate to 1 half of dough; mix until well blended. Divide each half into 2 equal parts. (You should have 2 white and 2 chocolate pieces.)

ROLL 1 of the white and 1 of the chocolate dough pieces into 10×8-inch rectangle on floured surface. Repeat with remaining dough pieces. Place rolled-out chocolate dough on rolled-out white dough; press gently to form even layer. Starting from the short side, roll up dough tightly to form a log; wrap tightly with plastic wrap. Repeat with remaining dough. Refrigerate 1 hour.

CUT dough into ¼-inch-thick slices; place on ungreased baking sheets. Bake 10 to 12 minutes or lightly browned. Let stand 2 minutes before transferring to wire racks. Cool completely.

Makes about 4 dozen cookies or 24 servings, 2 cookies each.

> *TIP:* These cookies are a great idea for a holiday party or cookie exchange.

BAKER'S ONE BOWL CHOCOLATE SWIRL CHEESECAKE

Prep: 10 minutes • Total: 3 hours 50 minutes (includes refrigerating)

- 4 squares **BAKER'S** Semi-Sweet Baking Chocolate
- 2 packages (8 ounces each) **PHILADELPHIA** Cream Cheese, softened, divided
- ½ cup sugar, divided
- 2 eggs, divided
- 1 **OREO** Pie Crust (6 ounces)
- ½ teaspoon vanilla

PREHEAT oven to 350°F. Microwave chocolate in large microwaveable bowl on HIGH 1½ minutes or until chocolate is almost melted, stirring every 30 seconds. Stir until chocolate is completely melted. Add 1 package of the cream cheese, ¼ cup of the sugar and 1 of the eggs; beat with wire whisk until well blended. Pour into crust.

BEAT remaining package of cream cheese, remaining ¼ cup sugar, remaining egg and the vanilla in same bowl with wire whisk until well blended. Spoon over chocolate batter. Cut through batter with knife several times for marble effect.

BAKE 40 minutes or until center is almost set. Cool. Refrigerate 3 hours or overnight. Let stand at room temperature 20 minutes before serving. Store leftover cheesecake in refrigerator.

Makes 8 servings.

CHOCOLATE-HAZELNUT CHEESECAKE

Prep: 30 minutes • Total: 5 hours 35 minutes
(includes refrigerating)

1½ cups crushed **OREO** Chocolate Sandwich Cookies
(about 18 cookies)

2 tablespoons butter or margarine, melted

3 packages (8 ounces each) **PHILADELPHIA** Cream Cheese,
softened

1 cup sugar

1 teaspoon vanilla

1 package (8 squares) **BAKER'S** Semi-Sweet Baking
Chocolate, melted, slightly cooled

¼ cup hazelnut-flavored liqueur

3 eggs

½ cup whole hazelnuts, toasted

PREHEAT oven to 325°F if using a silver 9-inch springform pan
(or to 300°F if using a dark nonstick 9-inch springform pan).
Mix crushed cookies and butter; press firmly onto bottom of
pan. Bake 10 minutes.

BEAT cream cheese, sugar and vanilla in large bowl with
electric mixer on medium speed until well blended. Add
chocolate and liqueur; mix well. Add eggs, 1 at a time, mixing
on low speed after each addition just until blended. Pour over
crust.

BAKE 55 minutes to 1 hour 5 minutes or until center is almost
set. Run knife or metal spatula around rim of pan to loosen
cake; cool before removing rim of pan. Refrigerate 4 hours or
overnight. Top with hazelnuts just before serving.

Makes 16 servings.

GERMAN CHOCOLATE CHEESECAKE: Omit liqueur and hazelnuts. Prepare and bake cheesecake as directed, using 2 packages (4 ounces each) **BAKER'S GERMAN'S** Sweet Chocolate. Cool and refrigerate as directed. Place ⅓ cup evaporated milk, ⅓ cup sugar, ¼ cup (½ stick) butter or margarine, 1 beaten egg and ½ teaspoon vanilla in small heavy saucepan; cook on low heat until thickened, stirring constantly. Stir in ½ cup **BAKER'S ANGEL FLAKE** Coconut and ½ cup chopped **PLANTERS** Pecans. Cool. Spread over cooled cheesecake, then refrigerate as directed.

ULTIMATE CHOCOLATE-CARAMEL PECAN PIE

Prep: 30 minutes • Total: 3 hours 15 minutes
(includes refrigerating)

3   cups **PLANTERS** Pecan Pieces, divided

¼   cup granulated sugar

¼   cup (½ stick) butter or margarine, melted

1   bag (14 ounces) **KRAFT** Caramels

⅔   cup whipping cream, divided

1   package (8 squares) **BAKER'S** Semi-Sweet Baking
     Chocolate

¼   cup powdered sugar

½   teaspoon vanilla

PREHEAT oven to 350°F. Place 2 cups of the pecan pieces in food processor or blender container; cover. Process until finely ground, using pulsing action. Mix with granulated sugar and butter. Press firmly onto bottom and up side of 9-inch pie plate. Bake 12 to 15 minutes or until lightly browned. Cool completely. (If crust puffs up during baking, gently press down with back of spoon.)

MICROWAVE caramels and ⅓ cup of the whipping cream in microwaveable bowl on HIGH 2½ to 3 minutes or until caramels are completely melted, stirring after each minute. Pour into crust. Chop remaining 1 cup pecans; sprinkle over caramel layer.

PLACE chocolate, remaining ⅓ cup whipping cream, the powdered sugar and vanilla in saucepan; cook on low heat just until chocolate is completely melted, stirring constantly. Pour over pie; gently spread to evenly cover top of pie. Refrigerate at least 2 hours. Store leftover pie in refrigerator.

Makes 10 servings.

SIZE-WISE: Serve this decadent pie at your next annual holiday celebration. Follow the serving size and enjoy each bite of this once-a-year treat!

CHOCOLATE-PEANUT BUTTER TRUFFLES

Prep: 20 minutes • Total: 1 hour 20 minutes
(includes refrigerating)

1   package (8 squares) **BAKER'S** Semi-Sweet Baking
    Chocolate
½   cup peanut butter
1   tub (8 ounces) **COOL WHIP** or **COOL WHIP** Extra Creamy
    Whipped Topping, thawed
¼   cup powdered sugar

MICROWAVE chocolate in large microwaveable bowl on HIGH 2
minutes or until chocolate is almost melted, stirring after
1 minute. Stir until chocolate is completely melted.

STIR in peanut butter until well blended. Cool to room
temperature. Gently stir in whipped topping. Refrigerate 1 hour.

SCOOP peanut butter mixture with melon baller or teaspoon,
then shape into 1-inch balls. Roll in sugar. Store in tightly
covered container in refrigerator.

Makes 3 dozen or 12 servings, 3 truffles each.

JAZZ IT UP: Chocolate-Peanut Butter Truffles are rolled in a
variety of coatings for a sweet treat that is perfect for gift
giving or for serving on a special occasion.

CHOCOLATE-DIPPED STRAWBERRIES

Prep: 10 minutes • Total: 20 minutes

4   squares **BAKER'S** Semi-Sweet Baking Chocolate
12   medium whole strawberries

MICROWAVE chocolate in small microwaveable bowl on HIGH 2 minutes, stirring after 1 minute. Stir until chocolate is completely melted.

DIP strawberries in chocolate, turning until evenly coated with chocolate; let excess chocolate drip off. Place on wax paper-covered baking sheet.

REFRIGERATE 10 minutes or until chocolate is set.

Makes 1 dozen or 12 servings, 1 strawberry each.

SUBSTITUTE: **Prepare as directed, using BAKER'S Bittersweet Baking Chocolate.**

HOT FUDGE SAUCE

Prep: 5 minutes • Total: 12 minutes

1	package (8 squares) **BAKER'S** Unsweetened Baking Chocolate
¼	cup (½ stick) butter or margarine
½	cup milk
½	cup whipping cream
2	cups sugar
1	teaspoon vanilla

MICROWAVE chocolate and butter in large microwaveable bowl on HIGH 2 minutes or until butter is melted. Stir until chocolate is completely melted.

ADD milk, whipping cream and sugar; stir until well blended. Microwave 5 minutes or until mixture is thick and sugar is completely dissolved, stirring after 3 minutes. Stir in vanilla. Store in tightly covered container in refrigerator. Reheat just before serving.

Makes 3½ cups or 28 servings,
2 tablespoons each.

DID YOU KNOW: In 1834, 86 years before the 19th Amendment was passed, Walter Baker hired two women to work at the chocolate mill: Mary and Christiana Shields. By 1846, there were several women on the payroll of Walter Baker & Company.

Tips & Techniques

Storing Chocolate

Store chocolate in a cool dry place (below 75°F, if possible), away from light, heat, and water. Chocolate should not be stored long-term in the refrigerator because of the risk of condensation; exposure to even small amounts of water will make the chocolate difficult to work with. At higher temperatures, the cocoa butter in the chocolate melts and rises to the surface, which causes the chocolate to develop a pale, gray color called "bloom." However, this condition does not affect the chocolate's flavor or quality.

Melting Chocolate

Microwave Method

Place unwrapped BAKER'S Chocolate in microwaveable bowl. Microwave on HIGH (100%) according to the chart below and then stir 1 minute or until chocolate is completely melted.

Amount of Chocolate	Heating Instructions
1 square*	1 minute, stirring after 30 seconds
Multiple squares*	1 minute plus 10 seconds for each additional square, stirring every 30 seconds
1 BAKER'S GERMAN'S chocolate bar (broken in half)	Up to 1½ minutes, stirring after 1 minute

When microwaved, the chocolate square will retain its shape. Chocolate will continue to melt after being removed from microwave. If after stirring for 1 minute chocolate is not completely melted, microwave an additional 10 seconds or until only small, unmelted pieces of chocolate remain.

All BAKER'S Chocolate except GERMAN'S.

Stovetop Method

Place BAKER'S Chocolate in a small heavy saucepan. Cook on very low heat just until chocolate is melted, stirring constantly. Remove from heat; stir until chocolate is completely melted and smooth.

Chocolate Drizzle

1. Melt BAKER'S Chocolate as directed above.
2. Spoon melted chocolate into a small resealable plastic bag; seal bag.
3. Cut a tiny piece (about ⅛-inch) off 1 of the bottom corners of bag.
4. Drizzle chocolate over desserts as desired.

Chocolate Heart Garnish

1. Prepare chocolate drizzle as directed on page 281.
2. Drizzle chocolate in heart shapes onto a wax-paper lined baking sheet.
3. Refrigerate until firm.
4. Place hearts on desserts just before serving.

Chocolate Curls

1. Warm 1 wrapped square of BAKER'S Chocolate in your hand.
2. Pull a vegetable peeler across the surface of the unwrapped chocolate, allowing curls to fall onto a sheet of wax paper.
3. Use immediately or refrigerate until ready to use. Chocolate curls can be stored in an airtight container in freezer up to 6 months. Curls should be served immediately when removed from refrigerator or freezer.

Chocolate Leaves

1. Melt BAKER'S Chocolate as directed on page 280.
2. Using a small clean pastry brush or narrow spatula, carefully coat the undersides of washed and well-dried fresh roses, grape ivy, or lemon leaves with a thin layer of chocolate. (Be sure to use only non-toxic leaves that have not been sprayed with any chemicals. Do not use leaves with fine hairs.) Avoid spreading chocolate to very edges of leaves.
3. Place in single layer with chocolate sides up on sheet of wax paper.
4. Refrigerate 15 minutes or until chocolate is firm.
5. Carefully peel leaves away from chocolate.
6. Use immediately or refrigerate until ready to use.

Desserts

Frostings, Jams & Sauces